Old G. I. s and Sleeping Dragons
By
Doug Francescon

OLD G.I.s AND SLEEPING DRAGONS. Copyright © 2003 by Douglas P Francescon. All right reserved. Printed in the United States of America. No part of this book may be used or reproduced in any manner whatsoever without written permission except in the case of brief quotations embodied in critical articles or reviews.

Cover design by Jeston Whitacre

In Honor of:

Waylen Powell
Joe McCurry
Arnold Palmer

And all the guys who left a piece of themselves in Vietnam

Acknowledgements

Writing this book means more to me than simply putting my thoughts on paper. Through these pages I have been able to understand why I feel the way that I do on nights when sleep won't come. I know now where the hate and the terrible disappointment come from. I know why there are times when I won't allow myself to be myself. Without writing it down, I could have never understood, much less found a way to cope with this part of me that I finally recognize.

There are many people to thank. First and foremost, I must thank my family who stood by me even though they couldn't understand my actions or moods. They have made me understand what love truly is.

A very special thanks goes to my wife, Pati, whose encouragement kept me on track.

A big thanks goes to my editor, Doina Horodniceanu, who made me see my book through a reader's eyes.

Thanks too goes to the commercial artist, Jeston Whitacre, who designed the cover, and never complained once about all the revisions.

My thanks and eternal gratitude goes to Dr. Douglas Ackerman to whom I owe my life. His skill make this book, and everything else in my life possible by helping me beat cancer.

For all those who I mention by name, please know that each one of you has my deepest respect. For the families and friends of those who didn't come back, I hope that this book will help you understand what soldier's lives are like when they are away from the ones they love. If any of the descriptions or accounts causes you pain, I am truly sorry. It was not my intention to add to your sorrow. But, I don't know how to tell this story without including all of its parts, and because it is about war, many of them are ugly.

CONTENT

Chapter 1	The Dragon	Pg.8
Chapter 2	The Cruise	Pg.15
Chapter 3	Rookies	Pg.19
Chapter 4	Suffering	Pg.25
Chapter 5	The Guys	Pg.28
Chapter 6	War	Pg.44
Chapter 7	Living In A Hole	Pg.51
Chapter 8	The Routine	Pg.55
Chapter 9	Homecoming	Pg.66
Chapter 10	Life After The War	Pg.72
Chapter 11	Finding My Way	Pg.79
Chapter 12	Special Info.	Pg.91
	Picture Pages	Pg106
	Poems	Pg.113
	Reflections	Pg.123

Preface

This is not a war story. Plenty of those have already been written. It's not an attempt to analyze the war and its impact. I'm not that clever. It's just a way to sort things out. After 35 years it still bothers me.

If you read it, just take it for what it is, a way to bring a part of my life out into the open. Maybe by doing this I can exorcise the demons that come in the night, mostly when I'm alone. If that makes me sound a little crazy, maybe I am.

A few years ago, on Veterans Day, I was invited to speak about the war at a local high school. It was the first time in over 30 years that a group of people asked me about what happened in Southeast Asia during the war. There were five of us in the room telling our stories, and I was amazed at how difficult it was. A couple of the guys broke down. One left for a while. When he returned he struggled, trying to make those who listened understand how war effects all it touches. We all struggled through our stories. None of us anticipated how that day would effect us.

The things that bothered us had been locked away for many years. Even though we tried to set them aside, and built our lives after the war, the memories didn't go away. They never will.

If any part of this makes you believe I'm feeling sorry for myself, then believe what you like. If the writing style is rough enough to make you criticize, then go ahead.

There is an attitude that war produces that makes vets different. It comes from being thrown into impossible situations where friends die, from believing that you'll never see home again, and from taking another persons life. All this happens to young men in their early twenties, none of whom are prepared for what they experience.

A big part of this is dedicated to the three guys whose names are on the honors page. They didn't have a chance to make the adjustment because they died in the jungle several thousand miles from home. They weren't fighting for a cause, or trying to make the world a better place. They were just trying to stay alive long enough to come home, but like so many others throughout the ages, they never returned home. They never had the chance to live the lives that all of us were intended to live. Their lives were cut short before the really began. For what? For life, liberty, and the American way? Was it to help those who could not help themselves? Were we in some imminent danger from the North Vietnamese and their allies? I've searched for honest answers to these questions so that I could find some justification for the suffering and loss of life. After all these years, I'm still looking, and so far have found none.

Chapter 1
The Dragon

There is a veneer between civilization and the jungle that is very thin. The human sole put it there, and it is the only thing that makes life, as we know it, possible. Without the protection of this thin shield there is no kindness, understanding, compassion, or love.

In a heartbeat, the blink of an eye, or the explosion of a satchel charge, the veneer can be shattered. I've seen it happen just that fast, and once it does, there is nothing left but survival by whatever means necessary.

It's amazing what humans are capable of when they're reduced to the survival only mode. I had no idea what kind of animal was inside me until that animal was released. I call it the dragon. It's an incredible ally, but a dangerous companion.

On the evening of July 3rd, 1967, we were setting up for a routine night, harassing the Viet Cong and North Vietnamese Army who we knew were in the area. We'd seen activity around our position during the day in places where no one should have been. We were in a pretty good spot. We had artillery support from 155 mm and 8" howitzers and air support whenever we needed it. The main drawbacks were the jungle that ran up to the very edge of our perimeter, and the fact that we'd been in the same place so long that it was easy to figure out our strengths and weaknesses, and determine exactly where to hit us.

And hit us they did, faster than I'd have believed possible if I hadn't been there. A full company of North Vietnamese Regulars and Viet Cong sappers attacked our re-enforced platoon. They were able to strike so quickly because we had no kill zone between the perimeter and surrounding jungle. We had no chance to react before they were all over us. We were immediately overrun.

That was the first time I met the dragon. I knew he was there because I'd seen glimpses before, on the football field and in fights on street corners. But, even then, it was only a glimpse. He was never in control until that night. I allowed him to be in control because I needed him. His strength, reflexes, and brutal determination meant survival. He created a feeling of tremendous confidence. His reactions were based entirely on reflexes. His decisions were determined by instinct. His concentration was total, and distractions didn't effect his judgement.

Simply put, humans are not that long out of the trees. In our basic form, we have every instinct and survival skill of animals that have never known civilization. These instincts and skills were developed over thousands of years of evolution, and they are deadly. In an instant I changed from an easy going, laid back, free and easy guy into a killer. And, the dragon and I killed with amazing coldness and efficiency.

We were able to push the N.V.A. back out of our position before morning. Through out the night I used the jungle the same way the Vietnamese used it to move in on us. Its thick tangled foliage became a part of me, and it saved my life. I wore it like armor, and moved through it as if I'd been there all my life.

During the clean up operation I saw a North Vietnamese near the landing zone where the fighting started. I don't remember anything about him. I only recall his image in the rifle sites. There was no hesitation on my part. No evaluation of his condition, or consideration of how much of a danger he still posed. I simply shot the young man to death.

I always thought taking a human life would bother me more. It wasn't what I expected. There was no hatred, not even anger. I reduced another human being to a problem that could be eliminated by squeezing a trigger. There was no kindness, understanding, compassion, or love. The dragon has no use for them because they get in his way. He was a brutal son of a bitch.

Generals, admirals, field marshals, and military leaders by whatever name, have known about dragons for as long as there has been human conflict. They use them with surgical precision. They are masters at putting young men into harms way, and turning them into killing machines. The United States armed forces does it as well as it has ever been done. They used me the same way that young men have been used since the beginning of time.

I chose to release the dragon. Even after seeing what he could do, I allowed him to stay in control. I made the choice between humanity and survival, and chose survival. God forgive me.

Over the years men have justified the rule of the dragon by saying that they had every right to survive; and, if the dragon provided the only means, then he was the right choice as an ally. I have used that logic for over thirty years. I've told myself that if I hadn't survived my children or grandchildren wouldn't have been born. I've also told myself that even though my contributions to mankind have been small, every little bit helps. And, in the grand scheme of things, I've done more good than harm. I probably got the idea from crap that some jackass once wrote, one who never saw young men die.

Don't misunderstand. I'm not apologizing for staying alive. I believe that it is the right of everyone to protect themselves. Even today, I wouldn't stand by and allow my loved ones or myself to be harmed. But, I've come to understand that if the conflict is intense enough the dragon will appear. There is a price for his services, and he will collect in full. I've been paying for a long time.

I'm not an expert on animal behavior; and I don't even claim a working knowledge of psychology. I only draw from personal observations and experience. I've seen cornered prey turn and attack with savage intensity when there was no place to run. I didn't understand when flight turned to fight until the change occurred in me.

It was dark that night on Nong Son, the kind of darkness that worked for cats, rats, snakes, the North Vietnamese, wounded U.S. Army sergeants, and anything that used the night time to its own advantage. There was no moon, the foliage was damp, and there was a breeze to help cover the sounds of movement through the brush. I was cut off from the unit and completely alone. Other guys were also cut off, and one had been captured. I heard him screaming as he was killed. There is no way to describe the intensity of the fear that I felt because no one has ever invented the words. It's pure emotion, pure adrenaline, and as basic as it gets.

The Vietnamese were so close that I could hear their footsteps as well as their voices. My rifle was broken at the stock, and I was left with nothing but a knife. That meant that I would have only one chance; and if I didn't kill the one who found me without any noise, one of the others would certainly kill me. It was hopeless.

Suddenly, the fear turned to complete calm. My focus was total and complete to a degree that I have never felt since. All of my being was dedicated to killing the man who found me. Nothing else existed, just me and the first one who came close enough. I sat completely still, waiting for my chance. The situation turned me into a killer, as savage and brutal as anything in any jungle.

The change was not due to bravery. In that situation there was no such thing. The fear was not due to cowardice which too didn't exist. The reactions were purely animal, and the animal's name was dragon.

Once the change occurred killing became second nature. Those who died didn't have faces. Any personal detail would have caused a distraction. Any human observation would have made the dragon less effective, and his only concern was survival. The rest didn't matter. That's why he survived.

Every moment of every day people decide which part of them will be in control. I believe that each of us has a compassionate side, one that is understanding, open, and kind. This part of us is in control when we are confident, secure, and at peace. As our situation deteriorates we begin to take a defensive posture. The worse the situation the more defensive we become. Since the best defense is a good offense, we may even take preemptive action.

True bravery is keeping defenses down in the face of danger. It takes tremendous confidence and self-control. The degree of confidence necessary comes from years of dealing with difficult situations. At twenty-one I didn't have that kind of experience or confidence. There were times when I set fear aside, and continued on in the face of tremendous danger. That wasn't an example of bravery, it was desperation. It was not difficult to continue on when there was nowhere else to go. And, the generals left us with nowhere else to go.

After we were overrun my commanding officer met me on the way back to DaNang. It was only the second time I'd seen him in the field since we arrived in Vietnam five months earlier. One of the vehicles was destroyed and a thirty-caliber machine gun was missing. Everyone in the platoon had been killed or wounded.

His primary concern was over the missing machine gun. He also wanted to know how the N.V.A. were able to get so close before the attack since I was responsible for perimeter security. I tried to explain that without an adequate kill zone outside the perimeter, there was no way to react fast enough. He didn't buy it. He was looking for someone to blame, and I was it.

That was my first experience with extreme self-control. The man will never know how badly the dragon wanted a piece of him, or how close I came to letting him go. I guess commanding officers understand dragons nearly as well as generals.

When people cooperate with one another, and give their fellow man the kind of understanding and consideration that's required, civilization works; and there's no need for extreme behavior. But, things breakdown so quickly that the best of intentions can lead to misunderstandings. Even worse, there are far too many people who just don't care. Worse yet, there are those who allow the dragon to regularly run their lives. They delight in the damage that he does, and seem to actually enjoy the pain that he causes.

They make such an unfortunate mistake because they never know the joy of a life where confidence, security, and peace dominate. The dragon has no place there. And, that kind of life is not possible while in his company. This is why he is such a dangerous companion. This is why his services exact such a terrible price.

With this in mind it's hard to understand why it's so difficult to keep him under control. Every day I struggle to keep myself from over reacting. I dedicate a tremendous amount of effort to keeping things in perspective. I do this because I know what is just beneath the surface. The most important thing is that the dragon can never come out unless I let him out. It's my choice, and I have ultimate control.

It's not a win all loose all, one time thing. Control is built over a long period. Peace comes from building a life where it can flourish. It's a simple concept, but a difficult life style to achieve.

Taking a peaceful approach requires tremendous courage and self-control. It means standing alone, and continuing on when support from others is not available. It means abandoning the security of the mob AND THE DRAGON even though their support carries the best chance for security.

My dragon's company will always be tempting because he doesn't loose. There is always an advantage to be taken, a weakness to be found, or an opportunity to exploit, and he is totally focused on finding them. He doesn't get tired or confused, and never hesitates because of concerns over others. But, dragon victories are short term wins, and never produce long term happiness. So, long term happiness is the price for his services.

I wish with all my heart that this world was a place where dragons were not necessary. But, it's not. The generals who put young men in harms way must use them as the line of defense against those who would rule by whatever means necessary to promote their own selfish ends.

Was this the case in Vietnam? Did we have no other choice? Was there a reason to turn me into a killer? Did I have to find my dragon? My heart tells me no, and that's the cause of my anger, resentment, and hatred for those who sent us there.

Chapter 2
The Cruise

There were thousands of us on the docks, all in new jungle fatigues with brand new gear strapped to our backs. We must have been the envy of every army / navy surplus store in the world. I looked in all directions, and all that I could see was GI's. I believe that each of us was thinking the same thing "what in the hell am I doing here?" It was the last time that some of us would touch home soil alive.

In front of us was the USS General William Wiggle, a liberty ship that was pulled out of mothballs, and converted to a troop transport. I was raised in the mid-west, and had no experience with any kind of large ships, but instinct told me that the Wiggle was a piece of shit. Once we got on board I found that my assessment was perfectly correct. Rust had been chipped off and painted over countless times leaving scars and gouges over the entire surface of the ship. It made me feel like paint was the only thing holding it together. The inside smelled like a basement, old and musty. Old pipes and wiring hung from every deck and bulkhead. They too were so incrusted with old paint that in some places it was hard to tell where one stopped and the other started.

I was told that the Wiggle had a sister ship that was torpedoed by the Germans during World War II. It sank in three minutes. Thank God that the North Vietnamese didn't have a navy.

My unit was birthed in the farthest forward compartment on the lowest deck, the worst possible place on an ocean going vessel. It was the part of the ship that rode highest on the crest of each wave, and dove lowest into each trough. The bunks were stacked four high, and there wasn't enough space to turn over without bumping the ass of the guy above me. There was barely enough room to walk between stacks of bunks. If we were animals, the SPCA would have tried to make these living conditions illegal. But, since we were GI's, it was OK.

The head (latrine in GI terms) was nothing more than a large lateral pipe with toilet seats attached to the top. Seawater was continuously pumped through it and dumped overboard. The merchant seamen had warned us not to use the first seat, the one farthest up stream, because in rough seas the flow changes direction. When it did, the seawater, toilet paper, and shit blew out of the first seat. I learned how important it was to listen to merchant seamen when it came to matters of seawater and shit.

The best defense against seasickness was food and a strong sense of humor. It sounds strange but it was true. The trick was to keep a little in your stomach at all times, and not think about how you felt. There was plenty to laugh about if you let yourself enjoy the show. Our favorite routine was watching the officers run for the rail when the weather got rough. However, the best special attraction was the army mule that an engineer battalion brought along. He was sick the moment that the ship began to heave or pitch. He'd hang his head between his legs, and make the most incredible sound I've ever heard. It came out somewhere between a moan and a burp.

The other on deck distraction was the flying fish. I was amazed to find out that they really fly, not very far, but it was definitely flight. Some guy who we assumed knew what the hell he was talking about said that they use this ability to get away from predators. I spent hours at the rail trying to get a glimpse of what was chasing them. It was amazing what a person would do to pass the time.

Below decks we had the continuous poker games. The guys who ran them would pay big bucks for someone to take their duty so that the game could go on. Some of them made small fortunes because the United States Armed Forces had the worst poker players in the entire world. There was no need to cheat because the average player simply threw his money away. It was a matter of simply waiting for a decent hand, and betting it wisely. The experienced guys would lay off one another, and rake in the money from the guys trying to fill the inside straight. By the end of the trip a hand full of players had a big chunk of the entire wealth of the ship. But, there was no real harm done because there was no where to spend the money, and no way to send it home.

Our only stop was Subik Bay in the Philippines for fuel and supplies. We were there for one night, and they allowed us to leave the ship. Everyone below staff sergeant was confined to the navy base. I guess they thought some of us wouldn't want to get back on board, more wisdom from the generals and admirals.

The only thing on the base were sailors, marines, and green beer that we drank all night long. I think some of it was still fermenting in the bottle, and later in our stomachs. It caused the worst hang over I have ever had, the kind that makes you think you'd have to get a little better in order to die.

To make things even worse, we hit a storm as soon as we left the Philippines. It was rough enough for them to lock the ship down and seal the compartments. It meant no officer at the rail or mule watching, and no food to keep our stomachs settled. There was nothing in the sealed compartment but sick GI's, and I was one of them. There was absolutely no where to find relief from the sickness, confinement, or terrible smell. That was when I found an incredible strength that has served me since that night on the ship, the ability to laugh at myself. I knew that I looked just as pitiful and ridiculous as the rest of the guys. I saw the mighty United States Army transformed into poor souls, any one of whom would have kissed a skunk's ass for just one moment of relief. I learned on that miserable ship that the sun would always come up tomorrow and things would always get better, another lesson that has served me well over the years.

I spent 21 days on the Wiggle, and would have been ready to get off no matter where it stopped. When we finally reached Vietnam there was no deep-water port, so we left the ship by landing craft. By any standards, disembarkation was a mess. The boats were World War II vintage amphibians. The best that I can say for them is they floated and managed to move through the water. They also got me to a place where I would spend the longest year of my life.

Chapter 3
Rookies

It's incredible that through the first several months in a combat zone I could have made so many mistakes and stayed alive. I am sure beyond any doubt there is a God because there is no way that I got through it on my own. There was so much to learn, and much of it was by trial and error. The smallest, most insignificant detail was often given priority over things that could mean the difference between life and death.

I learned quickly to respect my elders. They were the NCO's (sergeants) who had been through war before. It was a humbling experience because these were the same guys that I'd looked down on as a civilian. I regarded them as those who were living off the government because they couldn't make it in the real world. But, in 1967 Vietnam was the real world, and they knew the best ways to survive in it. They made the first order of business staying alive because a dead hero makes a lousy soldier. By watching them I learned when it was OK to relax a little, and when it was essential to stay sharp. I learned to judge people based on their character and values. Most important, I learned who to trust. I owe my life to those crusty old bastards.

When I think of them, one stands out among all of the others, Sgt. Williams. He was a career soldier on his second tour in Vietnam. One night after my section was overrun I talked with him about the war and our situation.

I said "God damn it Sarge, my whole section was killed along with most of the rest of the platoon, the mortar sections, and the medics. By the time it was over we killed, wounded, and scattered an entire company of North Vietnamese. By the next night we were back on the hill, and nothing had changed. What the fuck did we accomplish?"

He looked at me and quietly said "Man, don't you think I'm scared too."

In that short sentence he summed up the whole miserable situation. There was no logic, no reason, no justification. He told me I was a fool for looking for them. He said my primary responsibility was keeping my men and myself alive. He said I should quit thinking like a schoolboy and start dealing in reality. He said all that in just seven words.

At first I judged too quickly, and gave my trust too easily. An example was a Vietnamese engineer at a mine not far from a position that we occupied for a while. He was educated, articulate, pleasant, an all around great guy. I trusted him because I took him at face value and didn't look any deeper. All of the things that I'd been taught to respect in civilian life, education, wit, confidence, and assertiveness I saw in him. He disappeared after we were overrun, probably because he was working for the North Vietnamese.

There were others who simply said what I wanted to hear, or acted the way I thought civilians in an occupied area should act. They lived among us, shared our company, helped us build bunkers and observation posts; and turned all the information they gathered about us over to the North Vietnamese. They didn't carry riffles. They didn't declare their opposition to our presence. The "crusty old bastards" never gave them their trust, and kept them from doing serious damage. Thank God for "crusty old bastards".

We constantly had problems with the jungle. It grew faster than any weeds I've ever seen. One morning I decided to cut back the area in front of our position to improve visibility. As mentioned before, the wider the kill zone, the better the chance to react.

When in the bush, the rule is to stay sharp, pay attention, and think! I did none of these. Instead, I waded into the green surroundings with the machete flying. The jungle was falling all around me, and I was on a roll. As I stopped for a break, I happened to look down, and saw a wire about a foot from my boot. It was stretched tight, and had been placed there for a reason. That reason was so that an idiot like me would hit it, causing one of the mines in the field that I was in to go off, blowing my dumb ass away.

Like I said earlier, there is definitely a God because there was no way that I got out of that minefield on my own. I'm sure that one of his angels, assigned to protect the young and stupid, was working overtime that day. Once out of the minefield, I tried hard not to be a fool. There is a limit to what even an angel can do.

One afternoon it began to rain. I slipped on my poncho, slid under a piece of canvas, and waited for it to stop. If you've never been in a country that has a monsoon season, you can't appreciate how ridiculous "waiting for it to stop" really was. It never stops, night and day, hour after hour, it just keeps raining. By the end of the first night, I gave up on staying dry, and concentrated on finding ways to stay warm. The mark of a veteran was one who didn't waste time pursuing comfort, but focuses on survival.

My first encounter with the local culture came right after we arrived in Vietnam. We were in an assembly area just outside DaNang unloading our gear, and getting ready to head for the field. I was in the latrine enjoying a mid-morning shit when Mama San (an elderly Vietnamese woman) walked in with her broom, bucket and mop. My first thought was "my God, I'm in the women's toilet". But I quickly realized that Mama San was the only woman within five miles.

She paid no attention to me, but simply started sweeping and mopping. I remember wondering what would be appropriate at a time like this. Should I shit, wipe, or tip my hat and say good morning? It really made no difference. Any one of the three would have worked just fine because in that part of the world, at that time it just didn't matter.

There were younger women in the DaNang area, particularly at China Beach. Some were very attractive and extremely available. They were called "skivie girls", or in good old American street terms, hookers. They were part of the China Beach full service program. It included a whole gang of Vietnamese who would fill a 2 ½ ton truck with sandbags while the skivie girls gave blow jobs in the front seat; or, would provide more relaxed services behind the sand dunes. The price of the package was two cases of c-rations and a couple of cartons of Salems. They were crazy about menthol cigarettes.

While in DaNang in late July, I was asked to come along on a sandbag-filling trip to China Beach. It was always best to take extra firepower along because guys had had their throats cut behind the dunes. I was more than willing to go, but not because of a chance to do the happy dance behind the sand dunes. The thought of mixing sex with choking on my own blood didn't appeal to me. Beside, they had varieties of venereal decease in Southeast Asia that they hadn't even named yet. I looked at it as a chance to get away from our base camp for a few hours, and break up the daily routine.

While the locals were filling sand bags I was sitting in the front seat of the Jeep. Suddenly, one of the girls, whose specialty wasn't sandbags, walked up. She was wearing a pair of hot pants and a tank top that looked like it had been painted on. She would have been considered beautiful anywhere in the world. She was not only a knock out, but also the pushiest bitch that I've ever seen, and not used to being turned down.

After the third NO she pulled up the tank top, leaned inside the Jeep, and shoved a condom in my face. I made my move in one motion. I pushed her out of the Jeep, chambered a round into the M-16 that had been propped against my leg, shoved the muzzle under her chin, and hollered "if you don't back off I'll blow your fucking head off". The only one more surprised than her was me. After she backed up I realized that the safety on my rifle was off and my finger was on the trigger. I had only been a few ounces of pressure away from killing her. That was the first and only time that the dragon surprised me. I slid back into the Jeep, snapped the safety back on, and tried to understand what had made me snap. The only thing that explains it is the fact that I was cornered and completely surprised.

Two younger girls who had been filling sandbags walked up to the Jeep. One of them pointed at the hooker who was walking back to the road and said :

"Skivie girl number ten" (as low as it gets).

"I no be skivie girl".

"I work hard".

"V.C. (Viet Cong) number ten".

"They need to go back home".

"We don't need V.C.".

"We don't need anybody".

I asked her what she wanted, what would make things better for her and her people. She said :

"Everyone needs to go home. Everyone needs to leave us alone."

I talked with her for about ten minutes. The conversation made me feel as relaxed as I'd been since I left home. She told me that she wanted to continue to go to school. Someday she wanted to have a family, and grow old watching them grow.

Suddenly she looked into my eyes, put her hand on my thigh, and said in a deep, sexy voice:

"Do you care for me GI"?

I looked at her in amazement and said "Is every female in this country a whore"? She smiled a smile that didn't fit her baby face, and walked away.

That was my first step to becoming a crusty old bastard. I began to believe that there wasn't one single Vietnamese that I could trust. I didn't look at them as people anymore. They were simply the enemy.

Chapter 4
Suffering

On July 4th a few hours before dawn as I made my way back to the top of Hill 300, the one called Nong Son, two Marines called to me to give them a hand. They were standing in the trench line next to the small bunker where mortar rounds were kept. There was a fire in the bunker, and it was partially collapsed.

As I got there I saw a third Marine lying in the bottom of the trench. He was in very bad shape. All of his cloths were shredded, and his left leg was mutilated. Nearly all of the flesh was gone from his thigh to his ankle, but that wasn't his only problem. His back was covered with pieces of white phosphorus. White phosphorus is used in artillery rounds and bombs to cause fires and terrible wounds. It burns whenever it comes in contact with air, and there's no way to put it out, and no way to remove it.

I got there about the same time as someone with a water can. We dropped into the trench together, and began mixing mud, as much as we could, as fast as we could. The other two started packing the guy in layers of the mud that we mixed. The idea was to keep air away from the phosphorus to stop it from burning. The problem with what we did was that it only works as long as the mud stays wet and flexible. As soon as it dries it cracks, air gets in, and the phosphorus begins to burn again. So, one of us stayed busy mixing mud, and another patching the cracks. In a short time the mudpack began to work, or the phosphorus burned itself out. Either way, the burning stopped.

Once the phosphorus was no longer a problem we had to find a way to get him out of the trench. This was tough because of the mudpack and his mangled leg. We had to keep him in the same position by lifting him straight up and out.

I went to the command bunker and found a blanket. If we could get it under him we could use it as a litter, and lift him correctly. As I dropped back into the trench with the blanket the bunker exploded. The concussion knocked me forward and completely disoriented me.

As I came to my senses I saw the guy that was helping me mix mud hollering and pointing down at the Marine at the bottom of the trench. There was a mortar shell lying in the middle of his back. It had been in the burning bunker, and was still hot enough for the outside paint to be smoldering. I picked it up with the blanket, and tossed it and the blanket over the side of the hill.

I stopped for a second and thought about what I had just done. Then, said to myself "nice going dumb ass, now the blanket is gone". It's amazing what ridiculous things pop into your mind at any given time. I remember looking down at the poor bastard in the bottom of the trench and thinking "man, he's having a bad day".

As usual, one of the guys covered for me, God bless him. He found a poncho to replace the blanket that I had thrown away. We got it under our buddy and lifted him out of the trench. As we did the bunker exploded again. As it did the anger and frustration in me took over. I laid over the top of our buddy to keep anything else from getting to him. I was furious. I remember thinking "God damn it, can't you leave him alone for just a little while. Hasn't he had enough?".

A few minutes later we got him to the L.Z.(landing zone). I have no idea whether or not he made it. But, if he did, I hope that he found nothing but happiness for the rest of his life because he suffered enough in that one night to last a hundred life times.

There are many forms of suffering. There is the noisy, violent kind that shatters bones and tears flesh; and there is the silent kind that comes in the night, in the rain, when you're alone, and can think of nothing but home and the ones you love. Silent suffering causes you to discipline your mind so that some thoughts are put aside. There are times when memories of home are off limits. There are times when you must be satisfied with only the present because it's the only thing that's available. The past and future must be ignored because they don't fit into the world where you find yourself. They are too beautiful.

This causes you to blot out love, warmth, and the best of your memories because the realization of being without them is just too painful. It's a terrible adjustment. It creates a cold, hard, impersonal environment, the one where the dragon lives.

As bad as this was, there was a much worse form. It was the one that touched the kids; and there were many who went through hell. Their lives were shattered, and they had no defenses.

While in DaNang we were asked to help a woman and her daughter who needed transportation to an aid station so that the little girl could be treated for a head injury. As we helped them into the truck I could only see that the child was in pain and very frightened. Later that day I got the details about her condition. As was the custom, the wound had been covered with human waste (shit), and maggots entered the open sour. However, this didn't prevent the infection from spreading; and the maggots followed the deepening infection. The little girl and her mother were going to the aid station to have the wound cleaned out and properly dressed. I was told that the process was brutal.

There is no way to rationalize a child's suffering. There is no way to repair the damage that is done when they are exposed to extreme fear, desperation, and pain. They will live with their scars forever.

Chapter 5
The Guys

In the units that I was with I saw a cross section of the entire country. We represented everyone from schoolteachers to gang bangers. We came from the north, east, south, and west, with backgrounds as different as night and day. But, the things we had in common far outweighed our differences. None of us wanted to be in Vietnam. None of us gave a damn about the local politics, or who was in control of a place half way round the world. We all missed cold beer, family, old friends, and women who could actually carry on a conversation ("Hay GI, suckie, fuckie, mighty fine boom boom" didn't count).

Even the meatheads and the ass holes became my brothers. We tolerated one another, cared for one another, shared our loneliness, and kept one another going.

My best buddy was a Texan named Waylen Powell, the most unmilitary soldier who ever lived. He had a rare gift for getting next to people, some he made laugh, some he made furious; but no one ever ignored him. He made me laugh when there was absolutely nothing to laugh about. He forced me to justify things that I had taken for granted all of my life. I'm a better man for having been his friend. He was killed on July 4th, 1967.

Waylen was average height, weight, and build with no outstanding physical characteristics except his smile. It was always there; and it said that he knew something that no one else knew, like he was keeping a secret that was his alone.

He seldom talked about home, but neither did I. That part of our lives was too precious, and too far away from the shit hole where we found ourselves in 1967. We stayed in the present, and kept the conversations focused on whatever bullshit that made us laugh.

We were on a smoke break, in one of those bullshit sessions when a satchel charge came flying through the air and landed in the trench where we were standing. Just before it exploded I hollered "Incoming", and dove toward to road. The explosion threw me across the road and into the brush. When I came to my senses the entire top of the hill was alive with small arms and automatic weapons fire in all directions.

I found my best buddies body the next morning. Even though there was nothing I could have done to save him, I'll always feel that I left my best friend behind.

Waylen and I were assigned to different units when we got to Vietnam, and hadn't seen one another for a couple of months. We hooked up at our base camp in DaNang for a three day, in-country, R&R (Rest and Recuperation), and immediately headed for China Beach where we mixed a little body surfing with lots of beer. I remember the surfing because it tended to sober me up. Everything else about the three days was a little hazy.

I was born and raised in Illinois; and the closest I'd come to surfing was listening to the Beach Boys. I worked my butt off trying to out surf Waylen; and if I had been sober I'd have probably killed myself. I was amazed at how quickly he picked it up. But, he was an amazing guy. By the end of the day there were dozens of guys in the water competing with one another for style and distance, and he organized the whole thing just for laughs.

I later figured out that our rotation back to base camp at the same time was arranged to make it easier to transfer Waylen into my section. He had raised so much hell in his own section that they decided to assign him to me.

He was a lousy soldier. He questioned every order he was given, made up his own mind about everything, and if it didn't make sense, he wouldn't do it. He was no easier on me than any other NCO (sergeant) that he had been assigned to. The first night back in the field he asked why in the hell were we going to be up all night when the rest of the ass holes in the platoon were going to get at least a few hours sleep? I said that: first, we were in charge of night perimeter defense, second, if we're going to be hit it would be at night, third, when it happens I'd rather be awake, and fourth, if someone was going to be responsible for my fucking throat being cut or my head being blown off, I'd prefer it was me.

That was the last time he questioned why we were awake while the other guys were sleeping. You see, Waylen was a lousy soldier, but a very good man. What I said made sense, and he accepted it because it did. He didn't do things because the army said so, or because I said so. He governed his actions by what his heart told him was correct. He was honest with himself, and with others. He accepted responsibility when it was his to accept.

The things I learned because of my friendship with Waylen Powell have stayed with me all these years. He didn't give his respect to anyone. It had to be earned with honesty and courage. I wish that more people could have known him the way I did. It's been over thirty years, and I still miss him.

Joe McCurry was a little bit of every guy I'd ever met. He was burgers and fries, and cold beer after the game. Having him around was like being close to a piece of home.

He was slender, built like a shortstop (a baseball player who is very quick and agile). He kept his hair cut very short when long hair was the style. He seemed to fit in no mater who he was with.

He was transferred to me when two of my guys were re-assigned to another section. The army shuffled people from time to time, trying to improve units that had problems.

Joe didn't complain about being in the field. In fact, he liked the change from the "regular army" style of life that existed in base camp. He never considered the extra risks that came from being in the bush. Very few guys did until they were hit or were close to someone who was. The first time Joe saw serious action was the night he was killed.

He and Arnold Palmer were assigned to man our only search light on the night we were overrun. They were scheduled for sunset to midnight. Powell and I planned to take midnight to sunup. We normally had two lights and a thirty-caliber machine gun manned all night long. So, there was never a time when we weren't watching the perimeter. But, on July 3rd one of the lights was out of action, something that seldom happened.

The machine gun was always set up at the landing zone position because there were fewer Marines there. We wanted our gun to beef up firepower at our weakest point.

We varied the intervals of the illumination missions (the times that the lights were on). We also mixed white light with infrared (light that we could see through special binoculars, but no one else could).

Joe and Arnold ran their last mission between 11:30 and 11:45. They went to their bunker after that mission, but before Powell and I relieved them. That was a big mistake because it was the exact time that we were hit. I didn't tell them to wait for us, but I shouldn't have to. They knew better. They were both very good men who simply made a mistake.

Powell and I were in the trench line within fifty feet of the light and bunker. I'm sure Joe and Arnold saw us there and thought we had them covered. The Vietnamese who threw the satchel charge at us had to walk past the searchlight. The mistake and some incredible luck allowed him to walk right up on us.

The edge of the landing zone where the light was located was at the top of a steep ridge. It was less than one hundred feet to the edge of the jungle that dropped away from our position. Even if both lights had been manned that night we still would have been overrun. The only thing that could have made a difference was a wide kill zone that the Vietnamese would have had to cross in order to get to us. It would have allowed us to use our firepower. We were so badly outnumbered, and they were on us so fast that Joe and Arnold never had a chance.

Arnold Palmer was with us from the time we left the states. He was one of the most single-minded guys I've ever met. All he talked about was home. All he was interested in was back home. All he cared about was back home. He never talked about baseball, football, basketball, or women. He didn't even bitch about the army, the rain, or the 25-year-old c-rations that we lived on for months at a time. And, in the army, bitching is like therapy.

He just wanted to go home. Everything he hoped for, dreamed about, or wanted for the rest of his life was right there. He found paradise; and was just trying to live long enough to get back to it. It's a tragedy that he never spent another day in the paradise he found.

The two guys who were transferred out of my section, Ertus Ford and Pete Terronus, were as good as they came. Both were confident, dependable, and hard working. They made running the section easy; and, at the same time, taught me lessons that have served me well for over 30 years. The most important of these was trust, when to give it and how to gain it.

My section was one of the best in the unit, and it was because I had the best guys. I guess the Army decided that I should share the wealth.

There was no way for a section leader, platoon sergeant, or anyone responsible for the actions of others to be everywhere and see everything. Therefore, there was no choice but to trust my men. The key was to be as hard working as my hardest working subordinate, to be as interested in them as I hoped they were in me, to care enough about them that they knew they could depend on me. It was essential to be on top of our situation. Each detail was important because if it effected my people, it also effected me.

It was not necessary to be the strongest, smartest, or toughest, but, it was essential to jump in and give it my best shot. Pete Terronus was a very tough, hard-nosed Latino who was used to hard work. There was no way that I could fill sandbags as fast or stack them as precisely as Pete, but it was essential to be next to him, sweating the entire time that he did.

Ertus Ford was a schoolteacher. He was not only intelligent, and well educated, but he could think on his feet, and was extremely street smart. I didn't even have to let Ford know what was needed. By the time I told him he had already taken care of it. I simply needed to communicate with him regularly so that everyone was on the same page. I needed to know what the company commanders, platoon leaders, and battery commanders were planning, and make sure that we were in the right place at the right time so that we didn't have to do things twice. My guys took care of the rest.

The pit fall in the situation that I just described was to become complacent and lazy, to assume that things would be taken care of because my people were capable. That was where honesty and hard work came in. A good leader had be involved enough to know what was going on without getting in the way of those doing the work.

My guys taught me that the key element was honesty. Without it, good working relationships were impossible. Actions that could have been considered manipulative and userous were very appropriate as long as the motives that cause them were not self-serving. A leader that did not manipulate conditions within his sphere of influence would find it hard to be effective. However, he had to keep his own interests in the correct perspective.

In the beginning my relationship with Ford was difficult. I was transferred into the battery where he had been serving just before we shipped out. He was in line to take over his section, and should have because of his unusually high qualifications. But, because the army was the army and because I had time in grade, the section leader job was given to me. He didn't go out of his way to make things tough, but he certainly didn't cut me any slack. He expected me to do the job that I had been given from the moment I took over. He forced me to be sharp at all times; and, in a combat zone, that was a good way to do business. To this day, I'm at my best when the pressure is on.

Without a doubt the most colorful guy in the unit was sp5 Witkus. I never knew his first name, and never heard him called anything but Witkus. He had the body of an NFL linebacker, and the face of a Mafia enforcer. He was a career soldier whose ability to get into and out of trouble was only overshadowed by his ability to get things done.

I got a call from him on the radio one day asking what I wanted him to do with the truckload of cold beer. At the time we were on a hilltop, miles from anywhere. Because I thought he was kidding I told him to bring it up so that I could sit in it for a while. Within an hour he rounded the switchback that led to our L.Z. driving a ¾ ton truck full of ice and beer. In all of my beer drinking days I never had a better tasting brew.

After my position was overrun I was sent back to base camp in DaNang to get patched up and re-supplied. One afternoon Witkus asked if I wanted to go into town. I jumped at the chance to break up the routine of base camp. One of our stops included taking the child that I talked about earlier to an aid station for treatment of a head wound. After his errands were finished we stopped for a beer. After the beer we stopped for a couple of drinks. Because one good drink deserves another, we stopped for a few more.

Sometime long after dark we stumbled out of a local shit hole, and headed for the truck that was actually classified as stolen because he didn't get authorization to take it before we left. He stopped in the middle of the lot where the truck was parked, turned and looked at me with those Mafia enforcer eyes, and asked if I thought I could kick his ass before he kicked mine. I thought about it for a second, and said that it really made no difference because by the time it was over I'd make his face look like ground beef. So, no one would be sure of the outcome anyway. He thought about it for a second, and began to laugh. It started in his toes and went all the way up his body. It was one of those infectious laughs that you just can't ignore. The longer it went on the funnier that it was. As drunk as we were, neither of us would have felt the effects of the fight until the next day.

We got back to base camp sometime before dawn. The C.Q. (Charge of Quarters) was waiting for us and woke First Sergeant Brown. He began screaming before he was close enough for me to actually see his face. I was in that half way zone between drunk and hung over. I remember that I couldn't understand much of what he was saying, but the overall meaning was crystal clear. I was an army sergeant acting like a dumb kid, willing to get my head blown off or my throat cut for a few drinks. The word fool kept hitting me like a slap in the face, and he used it over and over again.

I'd been chewed out before, but never better than by Sergeant Brown. He knew how to make the words stick; and the "crusty old bastard" drove the point home. It was the last time I took a drink while I was in country.

My second best ass chewing came at the hands of a Gunnery Sergeant at the firebase at An Hoa. He called me in to tell me that I would no longer be allowed to use our jeeps to make our regular chow runs (going to get something to eat). He thought it was bad for moral because not everyone got to ride.

I explained to him that we gave rides to as many guys as we could fit on the jeeps; and it was better to run the vehicles up and down the road, rather than letting them sit in the same positions for long periods of time. I was being honest about the whole thing. I really felt that it was better to use them whenever we could.

He cut me off, and said that he'd made up his mind, and that was that. I cut him off, and said that those were U.S. Army jeeps, not

Marine Corps. I then reminded him that they were my responsibility and, as such, I'd decide how they were used. I finished up by saying that I really couldn't help it if he had a fucking morale problem.

I'll never forget the look on his face. Obviously, no other E-5 sergeant had ever talked to him that way. His face turned a color that I'd never seen before. The veins in his neck not only began to bulge, but I could actually see them throb. I missed part of what he said because those throbbing veins fascinated me. The one thing that struck home was the fact that he was going to call First Sergeant Brown about the problem. I really didn't want another session with the champion of the ass chewers.

Never the less, I held my ground, and continued to use the jeeps. Apparently, Sergeant Brown agreed with me because I never heard any more about jeeps.

WAYLEN AND THE KIDS AT THE RIVER
This is the way I'll remember him. He had a way of touching everyone he met. He was a very special man.

WAITING TO CROSS THE RIVER
ON THE WAY TO NONG SON
It was a one way trip for most of us.

HE'S HOLDING A LIZARD. IT WAS HIS PRIDE AND JOY.

ON CONVOY IN THE MOUNTAINS
There were two kinds of roads, muddy and dusty. The same road could be either depending on the weather.

PETE AND ME FILLING SAND BAGS
If we weren't digging we were filling.

JOE TAKING A BREAK OUTSIDE THE BUNKER
He's sitting on the spot where Pete killed the Bamboo Viper (a very deadly snake). It was living in the bunker when we moved in.

FORD WITH HIS OWN SECTION AT THE BRIDGE
No man ever deserved a promotion more.

Chapter 6
War

There is nothing more destructive, nothing more wasteful, nothing that causes more human suffering than modern warfare. Even the greatest natural disasters pale in comparison to the devastation caused by human conflict. Man spends generations building great civilizations, and then tears them to pieces. My dragon is only one of millions that wait for a chance to take control.

I understand where mine came from, and why I released him. I have learned that the only way to control the dragon is to control the situation.

I will always have a breaking point. There will always be a situation that will push me over the edge. I must use whatever is necessary to make my environment a place where the dragon doesn't fit. If enough of us don't make the effort, and recognize the potential for destruction; then even the most natural chain of events can lead to disaster.

It's natural for groups to form, made up of those with common interests. These groups can grow into powerful organizations with significant influence. Influential organizations with similar goals form coalitions with even more power. Eventually mighty nations are born. When mighty nations find themselves at odds with one another, then the stage is set for destruction.

There was a time in the late 1930's when World War II became inevitable. After John Kennedy was killed there was no way to stop the Vietnam War from running it's full course. There have been times throughout recorded history when mankind reached a point when war couldn't be stopped. The trick is to avoid that point, but mankind still isn't able to do it.

Man is not ready to trust his fellow man; and, with good reason. In the past one hundred years alone the world has seen monsters coming to power, men like Joseph Stalin, Adolf Hitler, Benito Mussolini, Maummar Gaddafi, Sadam Hussein, and Osama Ben Laden. Once men like these took control, and began to promote their objectives, there was no choice but to counter their actions with massive military force.

It falls to each man and woman to watch their leadership carefully. Pay attention to the policies that your government enacts. Ask yourself if all those under its influence are being treated fairly. Ask yourself if the wealth is being distributed evenly. Find out if neighboring nations are being treated with respect. Check your home as well as your federal government, your work place as well as your state legislature, your neighborhood as well as your city hall. If things don't feel right then they're probably not.

Keep in mind that there is always a way to make the situation better and less volatile. Most of the time it won't be possible to solve problems immediately. They're too complex. It takes time, courage, perseverance, and sacrifice. Understand that the costs will be high. Powerful organizations don't like opposition, and they don't play fair.

Above all be honest with yourself. Don't let your own selfish motives make you part of the problem rather than an aid to a solution. Ask the same questions of yourself as you ask of those who govern:

Do I treat my fellow man fairly?

Do I take advantage of those who are vulnerable in order to enhance my own position without regard for their condition?

Do I help when I can without the promise of future benefits?

My earlier list of monsters didn't include any Americans. Throughout our relatively short history we've had our share.

Every minority and native American group, including immigrants of all races and nationalities, have suffered because of them. Their influence has been generally limited, but has briefly found its way to the national level. If, for example, you believe that a single maniac with a cheap rifle killed John Kennedy, then you're not being honest with yourself. Why was the full content of the report from the Warren Commission kept under wraps for so long? Why was the investigation handled so poorly? How was it possible for the man with the most first hand information to be killed while he was surrounded by police officers? These are the types of questions that a truly civilized nation cannot allow to go unanswered.

This isn't about the Kennedy assassination. I only use it as an example of what can happen in a country that we assume is moral and civilized. We, naturally, want to believe the best about ourselves and those who we allow to lead us. But, each one of us is only human with all of the weaknesses and shortcomings that stand in the way of life as it should be lived.

These human flaws can cause leaders to make bad decisions. If bad decisions lead to poor leadership, then there must be checks and balances to either change leaderships' course, or change the leadership. We have such checks and balances in this country, and they work well when used properly. But, they can't work unless enough of the population is involved. A very wise man once said "You can fool all of the people some of the time and some of the people all of the time. But you can't fool all of the people all of the time."

Unfortunately, people allow themselves to be led when they see what they want to see. Hitler led Germany into ruin because the Germans wanted to be fooled.

Once war begins it will always run its course. Neither side will back down until there is no choice. In the mean time thousands suffer.

We find ourselves on this road to destruction for various reasons. Dangerous men gain control and must be stopped, nations with limited resources attack their neighbors and take what they need, those with strong ideals or convictions attack those who have different views, to mention just a few. However, only when people's survival is threatened can they justify making war on their fellow man.

Once war begins there is only one way to fight it, with complete commitment to destroying the enemy. As terrible as it is, it's the only thing that can shorten the horror. It's also what makes nations avoid conflict in the first place. This country failed in Vietnam because it lacked resolve. It sent its young men and women to suffer and die without being committed to swift and complete victory. Thousands died on both sides because we tried to fight a limited war when there is no such thing. The immediate task in any war is to kill as many of the enemy as quickly as possible, thereby preventing your allies and comrades from being killed. The long-term task is to damage the enemy's resources and infrastructure so that he can no longer wage war.

We had the ability to crush the V.C. and North Vietnamese and didn't use it. We controlled the air, the sea, and whatever piece of land we decided to take. They threw everything that they had at us in 1968, and failed militarily, not being able to hold or control anything long-term. Here's my personal account of how we limited ourselves.

My first assignment was to take a search light section to an outpost between DaNang and the Laotian boarder. It was located on a hilltop overlooking a river valley and village. It was an excellent place to control the entire area below. There was an adjoining valley that ran from the river toward the border. The river ran to the coast, and emptied into the sea just outside DaNang.

The valley that connected the river with the area adjoining Laos was called Antenna Valley because of the number of Marine radio operators that had been killed or wounded there. It was classified as an N.V.A. regimental assembly area although I doubt that there was ever a full regiment there. None-the-less, it was a natural highway from Laos to a number of areas in South Vietnam. I'm certain that the N.V.A. used it extensively. Lt. Mike Litwin, a platoon leader involved in an operation through nearly the full length of the valley said that he and his unit found a huge rice cash there, enough to feed a regiment. That amount of food was of great value, and would only be left in an area where there would be large troop concentrations.

Minh Hoa village just down river from our position was called "V.C. Ville." Because of the regular Viet Cong activity there. The Marines had occupied it countless times only to have the N.V.A. and V.C. move back in as soon as they left. We'd have saved lives on both sides by moving the civilians out and leveling it.

The tactical importance of hill 300, my first outpost, was tremendous. It was at the crossroads of the natural highways that lead from the north. It overlooked an integral part of the supply lines that fed the N.V.A. and V.C.. We had a chance to choke it off, or even cut it entirely, and didn't.

We were set up to hit Antenna Valley, any point on or along the river, or the village with artillery or air strikes any time we needed. The whole area was within range of the artillery base at An Hoe that had 105, 155, and 8" howitzers. In addition, we had 4.2" mortars and a 106 recoilless riffle on top of the hill. Our firepower potential was tremendous.

Furthermore, we had artillery experts in the unit. I was one of them. Before being transferred to a searchlight section in the 29th artillery, I taught classes on all aspects of fire direction at the army's artillery school at Ft. Sill Oklahoma for a full year. In addition to teaching I participated in live firing exercises twice each month. I knew how to precisely hit targets, and could have done so at any time during our stay on the hill. This was our advantage, tremendous firepower, and the ability to use it effectively.

"Charlie" (the North Vietnamese and Viet Cong) countered this advantage by operating at night. That was his time to rule. Our answer could have been and should have been strategies and technologies designed for night fighting like the searchlights. They were not only powerful enough to light up any part of the valley, but also had infrared capabilities. That meant that in most cases, we could see them, but they couldn't see us. We had snipers equipped with Starlight rifles scopes designed to pick up targets on the darkest of nights.

The only thing missing was practice. We should have conducted massive nighttime operations. Only then could we fine tune the skills, and develop the coordination necessary to take control of the nighttime. Instead, we only took defensive action at night. We never used the unit's offensive capabilities because we weren't allowed to try. So, during the day, we kicked Charlie's ass, and at night, he kicked ours. The stalemate went on year after bloody year.

The North Vietnamese and Viet Cong were "a one trick pony", only capable of a single style of fighting. Their success depended on being able to move troops and equipment without being seen. We allowed them to bring the fight to us after dark. They picked the times, the places, and the circumstances, which put us at a tremendous disadvantage.

We were badly outnumbered the night we were overrun, and taken completely by surprise. We never should have allowed that to happen. We had the capability to stop it, but didn't. I blame the losses on leadership's mistakes, and include myself because I was in charge of the searchlight section.

We should have taken an aggressive approach to our defense on Nong Son. In fact, we shouldn't have considered it a defensive position in the first place. It should have been a base for offensive action. If we'd have been active around the hilltop that night we wouldn't have been surprised. We could have brought our firepower to bear early enough to keep them off of us.

I won't argue whether or not we should have been in Vietnam in the first place. That argument will never be settled. My point is this, once committed to war, there is no choice but to make the commitment total. It's a very messy business. It's about killing, and there's no way to make it anything but brutal. It's not about pins in a map or numbers on sheets of paper. It's about blowing a hole in someone large enough so that the bleeding can't be stopped and that person dies. If that sickens you, then maybe you understand war a little better.

If not I'll explain it further. Civilians are crippled and killed, including children. The best of a nation's youth die before their lives truly start. They will never know the joy of watching their own children grow up, or have the pleasure of reading a story to their grandchildren. Resources that could be spent on medicine and education are used to produce tools that maim and destroy. Mothers and fathers receive word that the sons and daughters who have been such a great part of their lives won't be coming home, and they will never see them again.

The decision to make war is the gravest and most difficult that any leader must make. Religious beliefs, political ideologies, or the desire for wealth or power can't justify it. It must be a last resort, only appropriate when the lives and well being of a nation's citizens are threatened.

Chapter 7
Living in a Hole

Humans are as adaptable as any species We fit ourselves into our surroundings with chameleon like versatility. We find a way to survive under the harshest conditions, and can tolerate incredible hardship. Wild animals are given too much credit when compared with us. When it comes to survival, we're the champs.

We have risen to the top of the food chain in every area of the globe, and we inhabit its most remote corners. We even find a way to survive on and under the great oceans where we are at our greatest disadvantage.

We're undoubtedly the most intelligent of all creatures, but that alone doesn't fully explain our ability to cope. There are other factors that are much harder to identify and explain.

Much of the time my guys and I lived in bunkers. They were nothing more than holes in the ground with re-enforced roofs, covered with sandbags. They didn't keep out the rain, cold, bugs, or the many creatures that called Vietnam their home. For a part of the time that Pete Torrones and I lived in one of these holes we were surprised that we weren't bothered by mice, rats, or other creatures that like dark, damp places.

One day when Pete was coming out of our bunker, he knocked over a few of the sandbags that lined the entrance. The accident uncovered a Bamboo Viper that had been living with us the entire time we'd been on the hill. That was the reason we hadn't been bothered by the local wildlife.

The Bamboo Viper is one of the world's deadliest snakes. If one of us had been bitten we'd have died long before help arrived. Even with immediate care it's doubtful that we'd have survived.

Living with this snake was like keeping a Cobra in the house, and allowing it to roam freely through out every room.

I have no idea how he avoided us or we him. Intelligence had nothing to do with it. We didn't even know he was there. We survived, but he didn't. Pete killed him with an e-tool (a small shovel).

Civilized man in much of the world has become used to basics such as hot and cold running water, electricity, heat, and plumbing. These are conveniences rather than necessities when humans are in the basic survival mode. We lived without them for our entire tour of duty, much the same way soldiers have throughout history.

We were provided some of the innovations of the twentieth century such as C-rations that we lived on while we were in the field. They're individual packets of various canned delights like scrambled eggs, beef stew, and ham and lima beans (known to every G I as ham and mother fuckers). My all time favorites were the B-3 unit, a can of cookies that actually tasted like cookies, and a small tin of peanut butter which, when the oil was poured off, fell from the tin like a cookie. At one time long before we ate them they were actually food. Problem was they were canned over twenty years before they were given to us.

When I left the states I was a slightly overweight 235 pounds. My in shape weight was 225. When I returned from Vietnam I was 168. The Marines said I was lean and mean. Actually, I was closer to starving and desperate.

A few times while we were away from base camp, they actually brought us real food. The best of these meals was steak and ice cream which was packed in cooler type G.I. containers, and delivered by helicopter.

The ice cream was half melted, a kind of cold lumpy soup. I believe that one of the mess sergeants made it from scratch, God bless him. It was delicious, the best I've ever had. It was just plain old, half melted vanilla, served in a mess kit to guys who had been eating out of twenty-year-old cans for months.

The steaks were delivered raw, and we weren't set up for a barbecue. But, there was no way that we were going to send them back. Someone found an old piece of galvanized roofing material that we laid over a small fire pit. As it heated up the zinc coating began to burn off producing toxic gas. This smoke is a real problem when galvanized metal is used to fabricate parts in manufacturing plants and on construction sites. But, apparently it didn't effect barbecues because the steak, like the ice cream, was delicious.

For GI's in the field, cleanliness wasn't next to Godliness, it was next to impossible. When it wasn't raining and muddy, it was usually hot and dusty. Because of the sweat, mud, and dust, clean cloths only lasted a few hours. And, once they were dirty, washing them was a problem. My laundry tools consisted of two five gallon cans of water, a garbage can, and some type of detergent (Cold Power worked the best). The washing process went like this:
    Place three pairs of dirty jungle fatigues, socks, and underwear in the garbage can,
    Add three gallons of water and a hand full of detergent (don't use all of the first five gallons or there won't be enough for rinsing),
    Stir with a stick until the water looks like thin gravy,
    Dump the gravy, and wring as much out of the cloths as possible,
    Put them back into the garbage can, and add half of the remaining water,
    Stir until more gravy forms,
    Dump, wring, and rinse one more time,
    Lay them over the Jeep to dry.

Showers were also tough because of no running water. Someone found a wing tank off a fighter that actually didn't leak. They mounted it on a make shift wooden frame on the steep side of the hill where our outpost was located. We'd pour in five to ten gallons of water, wait for the sun to heat it up a little, and enjoy. It worked great until the spring monsoon washed the whole thing down the hillside. After that, we'd simply rinse off out of whatever would hold soap and water.

I only shaved when my beard became uncomfortable. Haircuts had to wait until I rotated back to base camp, and that could take months. Our longest stay in the bush was three months. By the end of that time we looked more like South American bandits than soldiers.

Chapter 8
The Routine

The armed forces gave a whole new meaning to the term boring. It could be almost maddening. The little things that were absolutely essential each and every day didn't take much thought. After you've cleaned a rifle or machine gun a hundred times in basic training, there was not much stimulation in doing it again. There was other gear to take care of, but it too had been serviced countless times before.

The surrounding area was much the same, particularly where I was stationed. Even when I moved from the interior to the coast, the effects of the change only lasted a day or so. No matter where the location, the routine stayed the same.

The warm, humid conditions were perfect for bugs of all kinds. Bugs like lights, and the searchlights were on all night long. I'm sure during my tour in Vietnam I saw every specie of insect in Southeast Asia. There was one huge red beetle that flew at the lights like a raging bull. When it hit it sounded like a golf gall hitting plywood. After the impact they would crawl along the fender of the Jeep like they owned it. We killed them by hitting them with the butt end of a bayonet. It was almost like cracking a wall nut.

Our day ended in mid to late morning. We never got to sleep until well after day break because we manned the search lights all night long, either on an out post or on the area perimeter. After day break the equipment had to be cleaned, covered, and serviced.

If we were lucky enough to be in An Hoa we'd head for the mess hall for breakfast before turning in. Considering that we were in the middle of no where, the food was pretty good, a real luxury compared to the C-rations that we lived on the rest of the time. It was incredible how good bacon and eggs could taste.

Sleep was different. Apparently my mind adjusted to my surroundings and conditions. If, for example the 105 battery that was adjacent to our tent, ran a fire mission after we turned in, I'd sleep through it. Keep in mind that 105 howitzers are noisier than any firecracker that you've ever heard. However, if someone walked into the tent, I'd be awake immediately. I guess the 105's were my security blanket. The same was true in the field. Big bore stuff didn't disturb me, but small arms fire had me on my feet in an instant. This was particularly true after I was wounded.

I was hit in the arm, back, and leg by shrapnel fragments. I never believed I could be killed until I saw my own blood spilled. That, more than anything else made me choose to let the dragon have his way.

We'd only get a few hours of sleep a day. At twenty-one I didn't need much. Once out of the fart sack (sleeping bag) the daily routine started. I'd check with the guys to see what needed attention. There was often something that needed TLC, and the work was normally assigned to the guy who found it. I can't remember anyone not reporting a problem to avoid work. But, as I mentioned before, I had a great crew.

One afternoon while we were stationed on Nong Son I woke a little early. As I crawled out of the bunker for some coffee and C-rations I saw the Marines in full combat gear in the trench lines that surrounded our position. The mortar batteries were fully manned and ready for action. There were F-4 Phantoms (fighter planes) and Hue gun ships (helicopters) overhead. One of the helicopters was painted red on the nose, and in the red paint were three white stars.

The whole scene was ridicules. Grunts (combat infantry and support troops) never acted that way in the field. As I stood there trying to figure it all out the red nosed Hue landed on our L.Z. (landing zone). A short guy, armed only with a .45 (military pistol) stepped out followed by a planeload of field grade officers. He walked past the mortar batteries and Marines in the trenches, directly to my position. There were three silver stars on his cap that matched the white stars on his helicopter. This was Lieutenant General Krulak, commander of Marine forces in the Pacific.

Unlike the Marines I wasn't in combat gear. My shirttail was out, my helmet was lying on the seat of the jeep, and my rifle was leaning on the front tire.

"Afternoon sergeant" he said.

"Good afternoon sir" I didn't salute. Saluting officers in the field was like hanging targets on their backs, telling any snipers in the area to shoot them first.

"How do you like the Marine Corps?" he asked with a smile.

"It's definitely different than the Army" I said, and we both smiled.

"Let me take a look at your equipment"

"Certainly Sir" I said as I turned toward the back of the jeep.

"No, no" he said, " they'll take care of that."

I stood in amazement as a colonel and major uncovered my searchlight and radio. As they did, the general asked very good questions about how effective we were at spotting targets, and how things were going from my point of view. He knew what to ask; and answering his questions was easy. He was a man who understood war. I liked him immediately even though I never, and I mean absolutely never, got along with officers.

He was one of the generals who put me in harms way. He left me with nothing to do but fight. But, I immediately respected him. Somehow I knew that he was asking me to do what he had done many times himself. I saw in his eyes that he respected me for doing a dirty job that he believed was necessary. He was a man who received respect because he earned it. I also saw in his eyes that he wanted to do more. He knew that we were limited by the politics of this dirty little war. The eyes of this honest man read like an open book.

My commanding officer came to the field a few weeks later. It was the first and only time he visited me on Nong Son. As he inspected my logbook he came to the note about a general inspection.

He said, "who came to visit?"

I said, "General Krulak."

He asked with wide, nervous eyes, "was the section in shape for an inspection?"

I knew where this conversation was going, and loved every minute of it. I said, "he only saw me sir, the rest of the guys were asleep."

His voice got higher as he said, "why were they asleep during an inspection?"

I said, "he didn't let us know he was coming. He seamed like a nice guy. We talked for quite a while."

He said, "were you ready for inspection?"

I said, "well sir, I did the best that I could, but ya gotta understand, I just got outta bed."

He was speechless. The man was definitely different than First Sergeant Brown who always knew exactly what to say at a time like that. He wanted badly to chew my ass. He wanted to make me understand how important a general's visit really was.

Maybe he read my eyes. If he did then he understood that I didn't give a damn about generals or battery commanders. And, I definitely didn't give a shit about what he thought was important. Maybe my eyes were as honest as the general's were.

On a typical day I'd head for the command bunker as soon as my guys were lined out. I tried to collect as much detail as possible because "who was where" made a difference. For example, some guys were good at being in the right ambush position after dark and some weren't. If we picked them up with the infrared lights in the wrong spot they could be considered targets.

Our searchlights were extremely powerful. When set to produce white light they could illuminate a wide area at great distances. When the infrared filter was rotated over the bulb the light was still powerful, but images couldn't be seen without special, infrared sensitive binoculars. Everything appeared as green shadows. The detail wasn't as good as it was with white light, but movement showed up very clearly.

We would pick up this movement when we switched for white light to infrared. White light caused anyone in the beam to freeze, and they wouldn't move as long as they saw the light. When we switched to infrared it appeared to them that the light was off, and they would move again.

We actually opened fire on two of our guys one night because they were in the wrong place. We intentionally fired high because we were pretty sure it was them. It probably saved their lives. One of the ass holes was actually mad at me the next morning for lighting him up. I told him that the next time I'd just blow his ass away. Actually, I understood why they did what they did. A two man ambush after dark is a very dangerous way to spend an evening. The place they picked was safer than where they should have been.

I often found projects to brake the monotony. One that took more time than I'd have ever believed possible was teaching one of the guys to back a utility trailer. It's a simple process that involves pushing, rather than pulling, a light weight, two wheel unit that turns very quickly. The trick is to chase the trailer with the jeep. If you want to back up straight, and the trailer begins to turn, you simply match the direction of the trailer. If it veers left, turn left, if right, turn right. In order to make it turn lift, steer right. Once it begins to turn in the desired direction, chase it in that direction so that it doesn't jack knife. It's very simple, but he just didn't get it. We spent hours going over the same drill.

I honestly looked forward to our sessions with the trailer. As much as I griped about how much time it took, it was the high point of my day, kind of like picking on a little brother. It was OK for me to hassle him about his trailer skills, but heaven help anyone else that mentioned it.

Waylen Powel was the champion of the monotony breakers. The guy could find entertainment in nearly anything. We were doing a routine river crossing on our way to hill 300. As we waited for the rest of the unit to close up, a Vietnamese kid walked by with some papers in his hand. Waylen said something to him in a way that made the little guy stop immediately, and come over to talk. It was different than the China Beach crew. The kid wasn't trying to hustle us. He wasn't looking for anything at all. He just stopped to talk to Powel; and in no time there were five or six more gathered around.

The papers that he was carrying were part of his homework. All of the kids had examples of work that they had done. The penmanship was beautiful, and the work was done in three languages, Vietnamese, French, and English. They were especially proud of it for good reason. It was incredibly well done for youngsters who were no more than twelve or thirteen.

It was great seeing that kids could still be kids, even in a hellhole like Vietnam in the 60's. Even there they managed to find reasons to smile. One of them packed a pet lizard around like a puppy dog. The damn thing didn't do anything, but seemed to enjoy the kid's company. The boy would hold it up by the tail, and the lizard would hang there, looking around like it was its favorite spot.

The little guy that I liked most was one who would come to see us at Namoa Bridge. He'd be there regularly doing what kids do when the weather is warm, and they have a chance to spend time by the river. I'd let my guard down, and allow myself the luxury of talking to him. He reminded me of me at that age when I'd find an excuse to sneak off, and hang out with the guys.

He was an independent kid, always alone; but, he never looked lonely. He wasn't interested in what we were doing, and didn't ask questions. He always had something on his mind. It might be fishing, the weather, or some animal he'd seen. We'd take a few minutes to talk about it, and he'd do most of the talking.

Those moments didn't last long. When they were over it was back to the same old shit. The army has a procedure for everything. If you looked hard enough I'm sure that you could find one for wiping your ass. And, regimentation doesn't come naturally to young men in their early twenties. My natural tendencies were toward "doing my own thing". I was torn between that and being a twenty one-year old "crusty old bastard". I chose being a crusty old bastard because I was responsible for other people's lives.

We spent a lot of time on care and maintenance of weapons, particularly the new M-16's. I cleaned and oiled mine daily. They had a terrible reputation for failure. The first models were very lightweight, and much less durable than the M-14's that we'd trained with. During the rainy season I'd spend even more time on mine, breaking it down whenever I could.

The grunts (infantry type Marines) claimed that they never had one jam as long as they used Remington ammunition. I heard it from several guys in each of the platoons that we were with. It's an example of one of the little things I paid close attention to during each day. My clips were always filled with Remingtons. I don't know how much difference it really made, but my rifle never jammed.

Another part of the routine was "fan firing" our weapons every day. We'd fire one or two clips, eighteen rounds per clip. It was a way to keep the ammo. Fresh and find any problems before nightfall. It also gave us a chance for target practice. The M-16 was different from most other military rifles. It was only 23 caliber instead of the usual 30. The rounds were very small which made it possible to carry much more ammunition. The rate of fire was high, so each unit had more firepower. But, the small, lightweight rounds were unstable. They would ricochet off almost anything. They were also less accurate at long range. So, I practiced on targets at three hundred yards. It was much tougher at that range than with the old M-14's.

As maddening as the routine became, it was absolutely essential in the military. The machinery and weapons were extremely dangerous. An M-16 round had such high velocity that a single shot could take off a hand, or mangle a leg so that it could never be repaired. Grenades and Clamor mines could kill and cripple dozens at a time. And, artillery and aerial bombardment if dropped in the wrong place could kill hundreds. So, to make sure that all of this high powered stuff was handled correctly, the military said practice, practice, and more practice. And then, do it again. It was crude, but effective.

I kept a log of my sections activities. It included entries on condition of the equipment, a breakdown of nighttime operations, and reports on our daily routine. There was a detailed spreadsheet that showed what areas we covered with the lights, and what we saw in those areas. I included registration points that pinpointed important locations such as river crossings, trails, and areas where we'd seen movement after dark. Registration points were important to artillery units. They were spots that could be hit with concentrated fire at any time that it was needed. They could also be used as reference points to locate other targets.

The kind of activity that we saw was amazing. One classic example was the boats that would cruise down the river right under our noses. They'd come into view, slowly pass in front of us, and sail out of site. We were told that they were fishing boats, and we were ordered to leave them alone. I've done a little fishing; and it was always my practice to return to the same place where I'd started from when the trip was over. These guys never did. Gee, maybe they weren't really fishing. What else could they be doing? You don't suppose that THEY WERE HAULING SUPPLIES TO THE V.C. AND N.V.A. If no one else reads this, I hope it finds its way to the idiot that gave the order to leave the boats alone. I'm sure that the Vietnamese that manned the boats are still laughing about the stupid Americans on the hill. If they read this I want them to know that the guys on the hill weren't stupid, but just following orders given by a jackass. They should also know about the countless times that they almost died, only because it shows how vulnerable people can be during a war. The dragon would have killed them, orders or not. A big part of my days and nights were spent keeping him in check. I'm still doing that.

Boats or not, the nights, like the days, went slowly. Imagine if you can in this day and age no ball parks, television, movies, nightclubs, restaurants, or public gathering places of any kind. The only relief was conversation, which in the service was called bull shitting. In its basic form, it was nothing more than the sound of another human voice. Even when that voice was telling a story that had been told a hundred times before, it still provided relief.

On the other end of the bullshit spectrum were the guys who make it an art form. They handled exaggerations, fabrications, and out right lies the way Da Vinci handled a paintbrush. They broke up the tension and boredom, and made the hours move by. The following is one of my favorite "bullshit gems".

Maniac in the Morgue

This guy on the ship with us took a summer job in the morgue because there was nothing else available. He asked himself, how tough could it be? It's not like anyone was going to give me a hard time. They're all dead.

He was responsible for moving bodies on carts from place to place and cleaning up a little, pretty easy money. The only draw back was the guy he worked with. He'd been working in the morgue far too long, and his habits were unusual. For example, he saw no need for a refrigerator because his lunch stayed fresh in the refrigerated drawers with the bodies; and he didn't have to worry about anyone stealing his pie.

One night "Mr. Lunch In The Drawer" took a new arrival and arranged his right arm, hand, and middle finger so that they were wedged tight against the top of the drawer with the middle finger extended. He then found our buddy, and asked him to check on the new arrival for proper identification.

A little after mid-night the poor guy opened the drawer just fast enough for the new arrival to flip him the bird. He said he didn't remember going through the door, or hitting any of the steps on the way out. His first memory was of himself standing in the middle of the parking lot, looking in all direction, trying to make sure that the new arrival wasn't following him.

The absolute best of the monotony breakers were the letters and packages from home. They made me believe that there would be an end to living in a hole and eating out of a can. They gave me a reason to let down my guard and think of better times and places. They allowed me to remember the people that I loved.

Even the packages that were damaged were great. One in particular comes to mind. My folks remembered that I was crazy about fresh tomatoes, and there were none better that those grown in the mid-west. So, they took a half dozen of their best, boxed them up in real pop corn for safety, and shipped them to me half way round the world.

When the package arrived it actually dripped a little. The box wasn't square anymore; and when I squeezed it the drip became a stream. One of the guys suggested that we squeeze it into a canteen and save the juice. As much as I love tomato juice, I passed on that one. Instead, we buried what was left hoping for a new crop of our own.

Chapter 9
Homecoming

America loves winners, but gives little consideration to those who fail. Very few pay attention to the winner of the American League pennant if the National League wins the World Series. The NFL team that loses the Super Bowl is just another football team. The fact that we sacrificed as much in Vietnam as soldiers in any other war, bled the same, were just as lonely, and fought just as hard didn't count. We didn't win, and were treated accordingly.

When the general public saw us getting off the planes as we arrived back home, we reminded them that the war was still going on; and their sons, daughters, friends, lovers, or they, themselves might have to go. We were treated like an embarrassment, someone to be avoided and ignored. I couldn't wait to get my uniform off, and try to blend in. But, that was foolish because blending in wasn't possible after living like an animal for nearly a year.

Very few wanted to hear about the war from someone who had seen it through a soldier's eyes . Walter Cronkite had filled them in on the evening news. They could detach themselves from the combat footage, but I was the real thing. I brought the war too close to home.

I was amazed at how many college guys wanted to explain the war to me. It was simple for them as they analyzed it over a pitcher of beer. The dragon and I stayed away from the college crowd, and drank our beer with guys who had less education, but lots more class.

One evening as I sat at a bar nursing a brew, a Marine in uniform came in and ordered a scotch and water. The bar tender informed him that they didn't serve service men in uniform. As the Marine started to leave, I stopped him, and asked him to join me. He said that he'd rather just leave, but I insisted. When the bar tender came by I ordered a scotch and water. When he brought it to me I sat it down in front of the Marine. As the bar tender reached for the drink to take it back, I reached for him.

He said "I told you guys we don't serve service men".

I told him "you didn't serve him, I did".

I made it even clearer by saying that "it was my fucking drink, I paid for it, and would decide who drank it".

The bar tender didn't say another word. He simply walked away. About five minutes later the cops came and arrested the Marine and me. WELCOME HOME GUYS.

There were many people who objected to the war for very basic, very honest reason. They saw it as a terrible waste, and sincerely wanted it to end. They weren't judgmental, and didn't try to convince me that their opinion was the only one that made sense. They were following what their heart told them, and I respected them for their honest view. My cousin, Nancy Oliphant was one of those with honest objections. She exercised her right to object, but still welcomed her brother-in-law, Jack, and me home with open arms. Her opposition was completely sincere, but didn't get in the way of her love for those of us who fought. That love was unconditional. She was a class act.

There was another very classy lady in my life during those troubled times. I began seeing her after my wife and I divorced. Our marriage was doomed by the long separation while I was overseas, my "go to hell" attitude, and her unwillingness to even try to understand.

This classy lady's name was Nanette Sheley, a nurse I dated off and on while we were still in school. Nan made it easy to relax and have fun weather sitting around a campfire with friends or having dinner at an up-scale restaurant. She fit in perfectly no mater what her surroundings. She was also very attractive with long dark hair and beautiful eyes. But, her true beauty came from the person she was. She combined intelligence with a great sense of humor, and an ability to make those around her feel welcome and comfortable.

Nan made it perfectly clear when I began seeing her again that she expected me to behave myself. Cheep thrills and one night stands were not her type of entertainment. She told me in a way that caused an understanding smile to form on my face that stretched from one ear to another. She tried so hard to be firm and kind, both at the same time.

As I thought about her no nonsense statement I suddenly understood what she meant to me. I turned to her slowly and said "Nan, I want you to understand the most important reasons I'm here spending time with you. Talking with you like this, having dinner, seeing a movie, kissing you good night on your back porch make me feel good at a time in my life when I have very little to feel good about. I can't explain what happened to me in Vietnam. Sometimes I feel nothing at all. Other times it's all I can do to control the anxiety, rage, and guilt. But, when I'm with you all I feel is good."

Times with Nan were very good. It was like turning the clock back to the period before death and destruction caused me to change, a time before the dragon. She made me see that my life still had promise as long as I held onto the good times and moments when the dragon was not in control. I tried so hard to cling to those moments, but they always slipped away. The war was still far too much of a part of my recent past. It was impossible for me to let go of its effects. I was so empty inside I couldn't recognize that I was falling in love with her.

Somehow she made me see that "the good times" were still possible, and that they would come again. Because of the time we spent together I began to see that somehow I'd be able to adjust no matter now long it took. Without that glimmer of hope

I found in the company of that classy lady I would have never seen that someday I'd be able to leave the jungle behind.

My down fall in many situations was an overpowering tendency to over react. This came from a need to be in control. I saw so many things that made no sense during the war that I came away trusting nothing. This problem hung over my head for many years, a constant threat to a meaningful relationship with anyone.

I wish times would have been different, and I'd have been more able to relax and let go. But, I had to leave Illinois. I knew if I stayed I'd hurt Nan the same way I'd hurt so many others that were important to me. I didn't even take the time to say good bye. I simply threw a few things in the trunk of my hot rod and drove away. I didn't stop until I reached the Pacific Ocean. It was a selfish, inconsiderate thing to do, but I was definitely in control, a paranoid fool in control of the actions of a paranoid fool, and the dragon was the cause of it. He allowed me to survive while in Vietnam, but cost me the chance at true happiness for many years.

The rest of my family tried very hard to understand. They wanted so badly to help put the war behind me, and get back to life "as it was". They couldn't understand that that wasn't possible because "as it was" was gone forever. It was a terrible heart breaker for my folks, and they never got over it. They divorced a few months after I got back after over twenty-five years of marriage.

I wish that I could have been more sensitive to the feelings of my family and friends when I returned. My mom asked me at one point if I still loved the people around me, and her question hit me very hard because it made me realize how much I'd changed.

I said to her "Mom, I don't even know what love is anymore".

I wish I hadn't been so honest because now I know how much my answer hurt her.

My dad, who in his younger days was an excellent baseball player, put a team together so that we could spend some time doing what we both enjoyed. The team never played a single game because I left town before the season started. I wish with all my heart that I'd been able to spend that summer playing ball with my dad.

I had to leave because I was hurting the people that I loved. I couldn't stop because by the time I realized what I'd done or said, the damage was already done. Each incident was another installment payment to the dragon. And, like I said before, he always collects.

My family members weren't the only ones who cared. I had two very close friends, Bob and Judy Blomgren, who tried as hard as two people could to help me sort things out. They didn't try to analyze or even understand. They simply listened. They were always easy to talk to, even before the war. I knew that they couldn't relate to the things that I said because war wasn't like anything else. They simply took the time to let me get things off my chest. I was blessed to have friends like Bob and Judy, two more examples of a class act.

When I arrived on the west coast, I stopped in Portland, Oregon, and stayed with my Aunt Rose while I looked for work. She was another great listener, the best of them all. The best way to describe her is to say that whether I was having the greatest day of my life of the worst, I always felt better after talking to Aunt Rose.

My cousin Joan and her husband Jack were there to fill the void left because my friends and family were now two thousand miles away. Joan is the kind of person that can make a party out of a root canal. She, like Waylen Powel, made me laugh when there was nothing to laugh about. Jack had just returned from Vietnam after being wounded in the chest and arm. He and I didn't talk much about the war. We didn't have to, and I can't explain why. Maybe it was just that we realized how lucky we were to be alive, and to have a chance to live a life that so many others will never know.

I spent my first year in the northwest working for the federal government on a survey crew. Much of my time was spent in the mountains and high deserts of coastal and central Washington. The work suited me because it was very physical. At that time I could have never coped with an office environment.

Not only did it give me time to begin sorting things out; but, also allowed me to see some of the most beautiful country in the world. The more I saw of Oregon, Washington, and Canada the more I loved it. Somehow it provided an escape.

I promised myself when I left Illinois that my life would change. It had to. The drinking, fighting, and "kiss my ass" attitude was turning me into someone I didn't know and didn't want to be.

I forced myself to quit drinking, at least during the week. Before I left Illinois I drank every day. I forced myself to walk away from fights even though the dragon loved them. I'm still amazed at how much satisfaction came from burying my fist under some guys ribs, or from seeing the cuts on my knuckles and knowing how much damage they'd done.

Whenever I walked away the dragon tore at me for days. But, it was the only way to gain control of my life. It was the only way to become the man I wanted to be rather than the animal I'd become.

Chapter 10
Life After The War

We are all blessed with the ability to block out painful memories. It's like administering an anaesthetic. Without it most of us would go insane because it takes a long time for deep wounds to heal, and we need a way to carry on while the healing process takes place. The toughest part of the process is during the times when the anaesthetic wears off, and we're forced to face the memories unprotected.

On a quiet evening in 1999 I was alone in our home in Vancouver, Washington.. Except for small, everyday problems, things were generally going well. The kids were fine, there was money in the bank, and my wife, Pati, and I were looking forward to our vacation. Suddenly, I felt that something was terribly wrong. My heart began to race and I started to sweat. I looked at my hands, and they were shaking. I had an overwhelming sense that I was dying. The only time I'd ever felt such deep desperation was in Vietnam. But I wasn't in Vietnam, or was I?

I remember standing in the hallway, telling myself to cut the crap and get a grip. I also told myself that this was the kind of thing that happened to neurotic fools, and I wasn't going to become one of them. Finally I decided that if I was dying then let's get on with it. That seamed to help. Maybe accepting the situation countered the anxiety, or maybe things just ran their course.

This was the worst of several such incidents. They always happened when I was alone, and never lasted long. They started thirty-two years after Vietnam. I can't explain why.

There were times during the war when I had little chance for survival and the fear was indescribably intense. Then, suddenly, the fear would disappear, and the dragon would take over.

During these times it was like I was separated from the situation, and detached from it. I was able to think clearly because fear didn't cloud my judgement. In fact, I thought more clearly, and reacted faster, and more decisively than at any other time in my life.

But the fear and desperation didn't go away. They were just set aside until later. The dragon was extending me a line of credit, kind of "survive now, pay later". AND, THE DRAGON ALWAYS COLLECTS.

The most important element in sorting things out was time. It wasn't possible for me to understand the things that I've written about in this book when I was in my twenties, thirties, or even forties. The parts that I couldn't deal with, I simply locked away. I told myself that I'd put the war behind me, built a new life, and that was that. WRONG!

Until a few years ago I was busy with family, work, politics, coaching, and a thousand day to day things that consumed my life. It wasn't until the kids moved out, and the pace slowed that the past began to catch up with me, and I had no choice but to finally deal with it.

The first step was admitting to myself that I had something to deal with. I, like all "baby boomers" who were raised with John Wayne movies and Green Bay Packer football, believed that the answer was simply to "suck it up". After all, that was what "The Duke" would do. It is embarrassing to admit that it took me thirty years to realize that "The Duke" was dealing with a movie script, and I was dealing with death, suffering, and destruction.

While in my thirties and forties I continued to play football, basketball, and baseball. During a Monday night pick up basketball game I came down on the side of a guy's foot and turned my ankle. I treated myself the way I always had by simply re-taping it, and finishing the game. By the next morning the pain caused me to see a doctor who put me in a cast for eight weeks while my hyperextend ankle healed. He also told me that my basketball days were over. According to him, the ankle had been damaged so many times that one more injury could mean that I'd give up walking as well as basketball.

So much for "suck it up". It was my first significant reality check. And, although a small one, it made me begin to understand that there were limits to what I could overcome by force of will. The time was right for that first step. The others would come later, when their time was right.

I've made many mistakes over the years because I wasn't ready to handle a particular situation. Most often it was due to a lack of experience. In a world where decisions were based on money and politics, the dragon was no help. Planning, finesse, patience, and the ability to analyze were the most important factors, and the dragon had none of these.

The anaesthetic made it possible for me to build a wonderful life with my wife, Pati. We've cruised the Caribbean, navigated the San Juan Islands on our own boat, played softball and basketball together, and built a relationship that made it possible for me to accomplish things like writing this book. There are no words to explain how much she means to me.

I've been blessed by being a part of the lives of our four children, and five grandchildren. I've watched Krissy and Kim grow into fine young women, and become great mothers. They both manage medical offices, and they're only in their mid twenties. I couldn't be more proud of them. Kim can light up my day with just a "hi dad". Her laughter is the most beautiful music I've ever heard. Krissy is my protector. When Pati is gone she watches over me, buys me dinner and drinks during happy hour, and smiles across the table in a way that says how much she cares. She holds a very special place in my heart. I played "strap on the gear, full contact, smash mouth football" along side our oldest son, Greg, he at guard and me at tackle. The game couldn't have meant more to me if it had been the Super Bowl. He's not only a great son, but 'also my very good friend. I wrestled with, fished along side and have had the privilege of being allowed into the life of our youngest son, Ron. He is very selective about who he lets in. I'm honored that he's allowed me to be there. I helped my grand daughters, Malika and Kaylee learn to swim, made them pancakes, and told them stories at bed time. Just hearing them call me "Papa" makes my day. My grandson's Grant and Dominic are old enough the wrestle with, and they do wonders by making me feel young again.

All of these things were possible because I was able to put the dragon aside, and postpone dealing with the past. I was also able to learn to navigate through the money and politics world where civilized dragons take a different form. They're more like snakes, not violent or physical, but very dangerous in their own way. The dragon that I found in Vietnam is no match for them in a civilized jungle. So, for life back home to be possible, the Vietnam dragon must be put to sleep. But, he'll always be there.

One evening a few years ago Kim, Greg, and I were getting out of my car a short way from our house. As we did, I saw two boys and a girl, all three high school age, arguing on the corner about fifty feet away. Suddenly one of the boys pushed the girl, and knocked her down. She got up, and walked toward me while the boys stayed on the corner. As she passed I could see that she was crying.

I asked ,"Are you OK"?

She said, " Ya, I'm fine".

I said, "I'll stay here and watch them while you leave".

As I watched them one said, "You got a problem"?

I said, "Ya, and you're it".

The one doing the talking turned to his buddy and said, "let's take him".

They walked up the street toward me, one slightly behind the other. I focused on the one in the lead, the same mouthy guy who was doing the talking. The dragon had already picked him out as the one to go after first. That's right, the dragon was awake, and in control. Vietnam isn't the only uncivilized jungle in the world.

Mouthy stopped just out of arms reach. The other guy was at his right about a half step back.

The one closest said, "This is none of your business".

I pointed out that, "I just made it my business".

The guy in the rear said, "She scratched me".

I allowed myself a quick look at his face. And, sure enough, there were scratches there.

I told the guy with the scratches that his damaged face didn't justify what I had seen on the street corner. There were two of them and one of her. As I talked to him I continued to watch the guy in front of me. His hands were at his sides, he stayed just out of reach, and his eyes and posture said that he wasn't ready for more than talk.

Long before they reached me I chose the best places to deliver the first punch. It had to be in a spot that would cause enough damage to put him out of action immediately. I couldn't handle both of them at once. So, one of them had to go down, and stay down.

This incident caused the biggest reality check of my life. While it was happening the dragon was awake and in control, but it was me doing the thinking. Or, was it the dragon doing the thinking. Suddenly it hit me. The dragon wasn't some demon sent to posses me. He wasn't some dark part of me left over from the Stone Age. THE DRAGON WAS ME, AND I WAS HIM.

It forced me to admit that I'm a killer. It was me who killed Vietnamese soldiers, not some beast from hell. I was the one that was ready to cripple the guy on the street corner, not some cave man. All of this capacity for violence was part of me, just as much a part as the guy who makes pancakes for his grandchildren. This honest look at myself made it possible for me to understand the events of my past.

I killed the N.V.A. soldiers that night because I wasn't willing to give them another chance to kill me. I asked myself if I should have taken more time before taking a human life. I asked myself if I was obligated to put their well being above my own. I asked myself if I had the right to be a dragon.

The answers came in a flash:
      Hesitating would have given them an excellent chance to kill me. They'd already tried once. I had no reason to believe that they'd changed their mind about wanting me dead. So, was it reasonable for me to take a chance? NO, not at a time in my life when I had neither the experience nor judgement to justify that kind of risk.
      Placing their well being above my own would have meant that I believed that saving them was worth loosing my own life. Did I believe that I should be willing to die for them? NO, I was at the beginning of my life with all of the adult portion ahead of me.

Once I had answered these questions honestly I was able to come to grips with my actions. I could look at what caused them, and decide if I believed that they were justified. Being able to do this has brought me closer to the kind of peace that I haven't known in over thirty years.

I have also come to understand my attitude toward the world around me, and the people in it. I have little respect for authority. I call no man sir. I do not depend on others to determine what is right for me. I'm fiercely independent. I take full responsibility for my actions, and apologize for nothing.

Authority over others is something more often acquired than earned. It is handed out as a reward for cooperation, an incentive for more effort, or as a learning devise for those who will some day shoulder significant responsibility. I only give my respect to those who have truly earned a position of authority. But, I do not regard them as one with greater worth than me. I respect them for their contribution and effort alone.

I haven't called anyone sir since I left the service over thirty years ago. Then I did it because it was part of the drill. I saluted the uniforms and insignias that the officers wore, not the men who wore them. I, like Powel, respected only those who earned my respect through their courage or effort.

Chapter 11
Finding My Way

I've always had the ability to focus on any given item, task, or situation. The war increased my concentration level .The classic example was the night on Nong Son when I was cut off, and there was nothing around me but the N.V.A.. I didn't make a foolish mistake or panic. I didn't give away my position by reacting too soon, trying to move when they were close enough to spot me. Instead, I focused on my only defense, waiting for one of them to come to me.

As the battle started the first explosion threw me away from the trench line at the edge of the landing zone and into the brush and wire at the side of the road. I was hit in the right arm with shrapnel, and my legs, hands and face were cut as I fell into the wire. My rifle was broken when I hit the hard surface of the road.

There is a period of time after the explosion that is a complete blank. I remember nothing about it. During that period I somehow made my way northeast of the landing zone and southeast of the Marine 4.2" mortal position. That put me directly in the path of the attacking North Vietnamese. I have no idea how I got there. Even in the dark I had my bearings. Southeast was down hill, the direction from where the Vietnamese were coming. Northwest was up hill from where the Marines were firing. I was pinned in crossfire between the two.

I only moved when the Vietnamese were pinned down. When they advanced, I stopped. They were all around me. Even though I couldn't understand what they were saying, I knew what they were doing because of the movement. It became obvious that I wasn't going to make it. The Marine positions were too far away and the Vietnamese were moving too fast and too often.

I remember turning to face the Vietnamese, and settling into a position in the brush. My hand stuck to the handle of my knife as if it was covered with syrup or wet paint.

As firing from the Marine positions died down the entire east side of the hill erupted. Explosions all around me shook the ground. I knew that this was our artillery from the Marine base at An Hoe. The only way they would fire on our position was if we were overrun. At that moment I was sure that I'd never live through the night.

I could fight the Vietnamese, even with just a knife. But there was no defense against the firepower of the Marine Corps artillery batteries. I pressed myself as tightly to the ground as I could and waited to die.

The artillery bombardment stopped as quickly as it started. When it did I turned east, toward the road. Suddenly, there were sounds of men running up the road, not NVA, but Marines. I jumped to my feet, and headed toward them.

They met me at the bend that led to the landing zone. I told them I needed a rifle, and somebody handed me one. As we came to the top of the hill I turned off toward the landing zone and my old position there.

The southwest side of the landing zone was very steep. As I looked in that direction I saw the silhouette of a man, and knew instantly it was not a Marine or one of my guys. I remember seeing him lerch backwards as I fired, and he dropped off the back side of the hill.

I turned left and headed east toward our searchlight position. When I got there I found the light that Arnold Palmer and Joe McCurry manned had been completely destroyed. I went to the northeast side of the landing zone and saw that their bunker was collapsed. Joe and Arnold were inside. They were both dead. I don't know if they were fighting from the bunker or just taken by surprise when the fighting started.

We spent the next few hours caring for the dead and wounded and picking off Vietnamese who were still on the hill. There were pockets of them in the trenches and in the adjoining jungle. Many of them were sappers (Viet Cong that threw satchel charges into bunkers and other fortified positions). Any that we saw we shot immediately. None of us were going to try to capture a sapper. They could still be carrying explosives, and we weren't in a position or the mood to deal with prisoners.

Many of our wounded were in very bad shape. One of the guys that I helped carry to the landing zone, Bob Bowermaster, was shot through the chest. This type of wound is called a sucking chest wound, and could have caused him to drown in his own blood if he hadn't received care while the fighting was still going on. Below is his account of what happened as he told it to me.

Bob and his fire team (four-man infantry unit) volunteered to man the LP (listening post) on the southeast side of the hill. He had enough experience to know that this was a much better fighting position than the bunkers inside the perimeter.

He and his guys pick up activity long before the fighting started. They could hear movement; and at one point could see small lights, like fireflies. It was probably the Vietnamese smoking drugs before the attack. Sappers did this to dull their senses because no sober man in his right mind would charge fortified positions the way that they did.

He reported the movement twice before the battle started, and was ignored both times. Powell and I normally monitored the infantry radio frequency, but our radio and searchlight were out of action that night. It was the only time in the three months that we were on the hill that we didn't have both lights working. The guys who heard the call explained the noise by saying it was rats moving in and out of the garbage dump.

When fighting broke out Bob spotted a big man, probably not Vietnamese, shouting orders to the NVA who were attacking the fortified positions. He and the fire-team concentrated their fire on him, and it took several rounds to finally bring him down.

Reinforcements from other units, artillery, and air strikes turned the advantage in our favor. As the Vietnamese withdrew they passed directly in front of Bob and his fire-team. He and his guys opened fire; and for a short time it was like target practice.

As soon as the Vietnamese located the source of the fire, they attacked the four-man unit. The Marine next to Bob was immediately hit in the wrist, and Bob called for a medic. As he did he was shot in the chest.

The bullet passed deeply into his lung. As he inhaled blood was drawn into it causing him to drown in his own blood. The only way to slow the flow was to plug the hole, which he did by sticking his finger into the entry wound.

Suddenly he felt himself being dragged down the hill by his heals, and it made no sense. His guys wouldn't handle him this way. Then two shot rang out, and his heal dropped to the ground. As he looked up he saw the familiar face of another Marine, Thom Searfoss, standing beside him. In the darkness Thom couldn't see the wound or tell much about Bob's condition.

He bent down to take a closer look, and asked Bob how he was. Bob grabbed him by the collar, pointed to his chest, and gasped a single word, "help." That's all he could manage to say. Even with his finger plugging the hole, his lung continued to fill with blood.

Somehow Thom knew what to do. He blew hard into Bob's mouth, forcing some of the blood out of the hole in his chest. Another Marine, Gerald Bird, helped Thom slide a poncho under Bob, and they carried him along as they fought their way to the top of the hill.

Throughout the climb they took small arms and rocket fire. One of the rockets hit close enough to knock all of them to the ground. Bob felt like the rocket hit directly under him because the concussion lifted him into the air. He asked Seafoss to see if he still had a butt, and Thom reassured him that his ass was still attached.

Bob was one of the first to be evacuated. Thom Seafoss, Gerald Bird, and rest of the guys who attended to Bob undoubtedly saved his life. Thom administered mouth-to-mouth at least three times as they fought their way up the hill.

That's Bob's story. Incidents like this happened all night long. The Marines that I fought alongside that night were among the toughest young men that ever lived. My heart goes out to every one of them.

Both sides, American and Vietnamese, took heavy losses that night. We slaughtered one another. The sticky material on my knife was blood. I was covered with it. There was so much on my shirt and pants that they were stiff. The blood wasn't mine. I hope I never remember where it came from.

I found my best buddy, Waylen at sunrise. He was lying on his back at the edge of the landing zone where the Marines had laid him. His dog tags (metal identification tags that all soldiers wear) were missing.

A Marine assigned to identify casualties asked, "Do you know who he is?"

I heard him, but just stood there. My best friend, drinking buddy, surfing pal, the man who make me look so deeply and honestly at myself was gone. Joe McCury was gone. Arnold Palmer was gone. All of the Marines that were with me on Nong Son that night were either killed or wounded.

I felt empty inside. The dragon was with me because I wanted him there. I remembered the Vietnamese soldier that I shot on the landing zone, and found comfort in the fact that I killed him. Waylen was gone, and now the dragon was by best buddy. I was a killer because that was what I wanted to be. It made things right. It made them fit.

After that night there were periods when I couldn't sleep. The dragon wouldn't let me. I'd think about how to position our M-60 machine gun so that we'd have the best possible field of fire. That would insure more kills. I'd check my ammunition clips over and over again, making sure that they were loaded correctly. I checked maps time and time again to pin down key locations and likely target positions. I ran artillery fire missions in my head over and over again. I became a little unbalanced.

All of this happened to me when I was twenty-one years old. It changed my life forever, and showed me a part of myself that I couldn't believe existed, MY DRAGON. When the fighting started none of my actions were planned. Everything was instinct. I truly became an animal.

Once the change occurred I was never the same person again. The dragon became too much a part of me. The only rule was there were no rules. I remember rationalizing it with the fact that I didn't create the war. In fact, I never wanted to be a part of it. Those who didn't have to see the blood or feel war first hand threw me into it. The laid back kid from Illinois couldn't deal with war, but the dragon could.

So, the dragon allowed me to survive. But, that's all it was, just survival. Dragons don't love, they don't care, they don't even feel.

Happiness was never possible when I was with the dragon. Something inside told me I had to separate myself from him. Call it a voice from my sole, my conscience, or God's influence on me. By whatever name it was unbelievably strong, and drove me to gain control of my life. But, wanting to become a decent human being wasn't enough. It took a war to make me an animal. It took a lot more than just desire to make me human again.

It was years before I found a way to begin. At first I just got drunk and caused trouble. I tried my best to stay away from friends and family when I was drinking. It was my way of hiding a side of myself that I didn't want them to see. Often it didn't work. Even when I was sober I hurt those close to me. When I was drunk, I was a complete ass hole.

After a while I realized that in order to control myself I had to control the situation. If I hung out in dives I'd get into trouble. If I had a couple of beers at a neighborhood tavern with friends, I'd usually be OK.

There were many times when I wouldn't allow myself to be myself. Often, I simply didn't think I could control a given situation, and would pull away from people, keeping them at arm's length. As I got older I found more and more ways to stay in control. I got out of union business, politics, and coaching, all of which produced volatile situations. I said, "kiss my ass" as a way to end an argument rather than escalate a confrontation.

As time went on I was able to go for months without having problems, but the problems didn't go away. Suddenly the past would come crashing down on me.

Call these times panic attacks, flash backs, delayed stress, or whatever, they were very tough to deal with. Even though I knew at the time they occurred I was in no danger, I was trapped by their effect. During one of these events I walked out of the house in the middle of the night in a pair of sweat pants in a rainstorm because it was the most effective way to break the effects of the event. The cold and wet helped bring me back to reality.

The key to coping was learning to relax. It sounds so simple, but was incredibly difficult. It couldn't be done by taking deep breaths, using today's fashionable drugs, or any other method that simply treated the symptom. The most effective way for me to cope was finding out what triggers the event, and dealing with it.

The tough part was, and still is that there are many triggers, any one of which can cause an event. It was very important to keep day-to-day things in order. All of the little things must be under control. The checkbook had to balance. The vehicles needed to run right. It was important to take an hour for my daily work out. It was essential to get away from the office for some fishing, or a cruise with Pati, or an afternoon with my family. If I didn't things would back up to a point where they became overwhelming, and the demons would return.

I'm not talking about little red guys with horns and pointed tails that poked me in the ass with pitchforks. These demons were a part of me just like the dragon, born of the fear that I first saw the night we were overrun. They came with the realization that the life that I held so dearly could quickly and violently end.

But, I've learned to deal with the demons much more effectively than the dragon. One answer came in a phrase that I heard many years ago, "A coward dies a thousand deaths, a brave man only one". It worked even though I've never totally agreed with the terms coward or brave man, and I considered myself neither. However, the idea fits. Why should I face death over and over when it will only happen once.

The demons still come, even when things are under control, and I'm ready for them. Our oldest son, Greg, asked me to go with him to see "We Were Solders", a very graphic film about the war. I agreed to go even though it was about a unit that had been partially overrun. I was very surprised to find that the graphic footage really didn't bother me. But the sound of the helicopters hit me like a ton of bricks. There is nothing in the world that sounds like helicopters. Hearing their blades brought back the site of each guy that I helped load into a Medivac.

By necessity I've become very deliberate in my daily routine. I take life one day at a time because that's the only way that I can deal with it. Often, one day is too much; so, I stay strictly in the moment.

The dragon feeds on fear, desperation, and hatred. I felt all of these in that shit hole where I was sent so many years ago. These feelings were not directed at those who I fought because they were sent by others the same as I was. They were directed at the miserable bastards who sent me to do their killing for them because all of the death and destruction was for nothing.

When I got back home I wanted to visit the families of the guys in my unit who were killed, but I knew that I couldn't look them in the eye, and explain what happened without the despair showing. I knew they would question why they had suffered such a tremendous loss, and I would have no answer for them. We weren't defending America because America hadn't been attacked. We weren't protecting our families or ourselves because we were in no danger.

We got into the war because this country's leaders made a mistake, and that proves that they were human. We stayed in the war because our leaders didn't have the courage to admit the mistake, and that's what caused thousands to suffer and die needlessly.

That's the root of my contempt for authority. It's why I spend so much time finding ways to hold back what I feel deep inside. I fight to keep these feelings hidden, and work at avoiding situations that will bring them out. I wish with all of my heart that I was a better man, one who could forgive and forget. But, in over thirty years I haven't grown enough to find the peace that would come from letting it go, and putting it behind me.

The thing that I seek most of all is peace. I want to sit on the back of my boat and watch the sun set. I want to hear my grandchildren laugh. I want to see my kids happy and secure. I want to walk along the bay in the moon light with my wife, and think of nothing but the lights on the water and the stars overhead.

If the people around me were asked to describe me, they would paint a far different picture than the man I've described in this book. What they see is the part of me that I allow to be exposed. It's the image that allows me to function in a world where I don't fit. I guess that this approach makes me a phony, even a hypocrite. But, it's been necessary in order to function in a world that would not accept the real me.

When I moved from Illinois after the war, I realized that my life had to change. The drinking, fighting, and "go to hell" attitude that had hurt the ones closest to me had to be tucked away. I couldn't leave it behind any more than any other part of me. So, I had to hide it.

This has caused considerable internal conflict, the kind that, over the years, has taken its toll. There are times when even a routine day leaves me exhausted. There have been countless times that I've walked away from situations when walking away was not what I wanted to do. But, the real me, the one I chose to hide would have over reacted, and caused much greater problems, the kind of problems that it took the police to straighten out in Illinois.

If I could only find the middle ground, somewhere between the dragon and the guy that has to walk away. I'm closer to it than I've ever been before. I hope with all of my heart that it's a sign that I'm finally letting go of the past. I want so badly to let my guard down, and allow myself to be myself.

As I look back on the past it alarms me to realize that the times that I was the most natural and effective were the times that the worst in me was showing. I served a term as a union officer in a pipe fitters local, and took to the job like a duck to water. I remember an incident in a hall way with another officer as we stood nose to nose screaming at one another, each ready to kick the others ass. I was completely at home with the situation.

During the same period I was the union representative on a construction site manned with several hundred craftsman. The company that we worked for had been in the business for a long time, and was as hard nosed as any of the building trades unions that it constantly fought. I adjusted to the environment immediately, and became a complete asshole.

That is not a part of my life that I'm proud of. It's not the kind of person that I want to be. But, like the demons and dragon, it's part of me. So, we're back to the choices thing, the part where each of us must decide which part of their make up will rule.

It's easy to be an asshole. All you have to do is drop the rains, and let the dragon run free. I have enough animosity inside to shit on everyone that I know a hundred times over. But then, I would see again the look in my mother's eyes when I told her that "I don't know what love is anymore". And, I never want to hurt anyone that way again. She had done nothing all of my life but love me. And, with one thoughtless remark I broke her heart.

Here's where the conflict gets tough. When I walk away the dragon scratches and claws trying to get out. If I don't let him out he continues to scratch and claw at me. If I turn him loose he'll always over react. So, the middle ground is essential.

I've found a piece of that middle ground by telling the world to kiss my ass. But, I have to be careful. When I say it I can't be vindictive or malicious. As I say it I have to let go. When I do the dragon goes to sleep. It sounds so simple, but is one of the toughest things I've ever tried to master.

These things help:

I try to "CRY A LITTLE AND LAUGH A LOT". I deal with the demons and dragon when I must, get it over with, and find every possible joy that I can after the episode is over.

I try to "TAKE ONE THING AT A TIME AND DO IT RIGHT. I won't allow myself to be overloaded. I won't make myself responsible for things that are beyond my control. And I put family and myself first.

I try to "NEVER TAKE THOSE CLOSE TO ME FOR GRANTED". My family, particularly my wife Pati, is the glue that holds my life together. Without it life would have no meaning or purpose.

I try to "TAKE PLEASURE IN THE LITTLE THINGS". I make the most of the little accomplishments that come along each and every day. Life's struggles will be with me always. I don't dwell on their difficulties.

I try to "PUT MY TRUST IN GOD". I could never understand how God and war could exist, both in the same world until I realized that war was man's doing. God cleans up the mess. In the face of it all I must have faith. That's my true test of courage. I pray that I'm up to it.

If you've never seen war, I hope that reading this has made you understand it a little better. If you have seen it first hand, I hope that reading this has helped you in the same way that writing it has helped me. For all of the vets who have done their time in hell, may you find your own peace.

I LOVE YOU GUYS.
Your buddy, Doug

Chapter 12
Special Information

There was a very special man, a Medal Of Honor winner, who deserves a page all his own. Every American who survived the battle on Nong Son on July 4th, 1967 was given his chance to survive by PFC Melvin Newlin.

He provided us the time we needed. If the NVA and VC would have been able to concentrate on the few of us that survived the first assault, we'd have all been killed; and they would have taken or distorted every piece of equipment.

Instead, they were so busy with Newlin that they had little time for anything else. I was in the midst of a full company of Vietnamese, over two hundred of them. I could move among them, and take them on one at a time because they were concentrating on him.

Like most of the rest of us he was wounded when the battle started. The medic (Navy Corpsman) estimated that he was hit nearly twenty times before he finally fell. He fired so many rounds so fast that his machine gun jammed when it overheated.

He was defenseless, and wounded several more times as he changed the barrel. With a new one in place he opened fire again, pinning down and killing enemy troops who had captured the top of the hill.

He gave his life for me and every other guy on the hill that night. I owe him everything, and didn't even know him.

PFC Melvin Newlin

Medal of Honor, 1967, United States Marines, 2/5/1 Viet Nam

Citation:
For conspicuous gallantry and intrepidity at the risk of his life above and beyond the call of duty while serving as a machine gunner attached to the First Platoon, Company F, Second Battalion, Fifth Marines, First Marine Division, in the Republic of Vietnam on 3 and 4 July 1967. Private Newlin with four other Marines was manning a key position on the perimeter of the Nong Son outpost when the enemy launched a savage and well coordinated mortar and infantry assault, seriously wounding him and killing his four comrades. Propping himself against his machine gun, he poured a deadly accurate stream of fire into the charging ranks of the Viet Cong. Though repeatedly hit by small arms fire, he twice repelled enemy attempts to overrun his position. During the third attempt a grenade explosion wounded him again and knocked him to the ground unconscious. The Viet Cong guerrillas, believing him dead, bypassed him and continued their assault on the main force. Meanwhile Private Newlin regained consciousness, crawled back to his weapon, and brought it to bear on the rear of the enemy causing havoc and confusion among them. Spotting the enemy attempting to bring a captured 106 recoilless weapon to bear on other marine positions, he shifted his fire, inflicting heavy casualties on the enemy and preventing them from firing the captured weapon. He then shifted his fire back to the primary enemy force, causing the enemy to stop their assault on the Marine bunkers and to once again attack his machine gun position. Valiantly fighting off two more enemy assaults, he firmly held his ground until mortally wounded. Private Newlin had single-handedly broken up and disorganized the entire enemy assault force, causing them to lose momentum and delaying them long enough for his fellow Marines to organize a defense and beat off their secondary attack. His indomitable courage, fortitude, and unwavering devotion to duty in the face of almost certain death reflected great credit upon himself and the Marine Corps and upheld the highest traditions of the United States Naval Service.

An Hoe / Nong Son

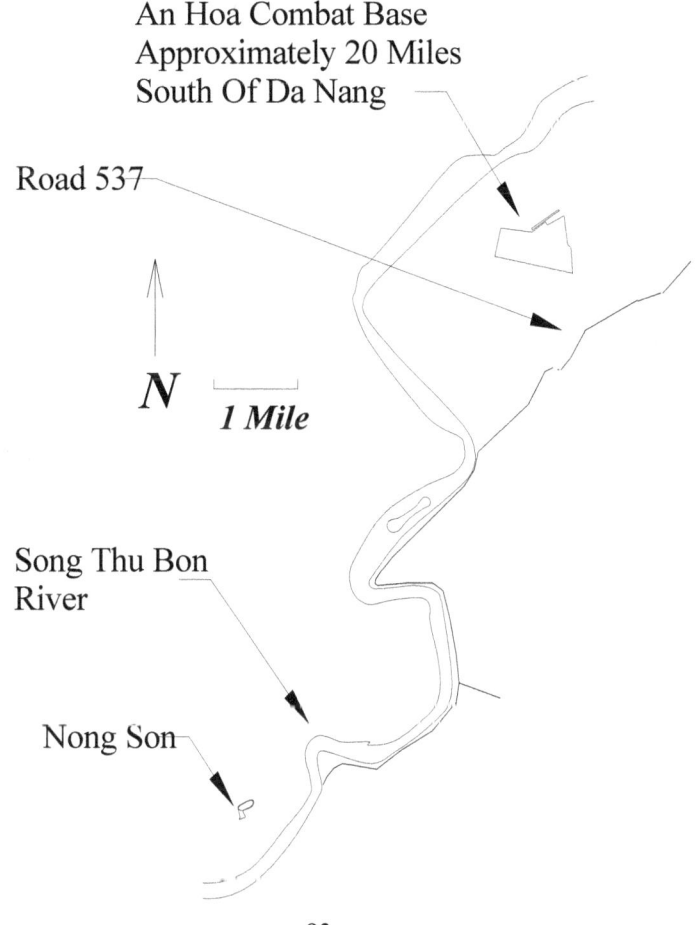

Nong Son

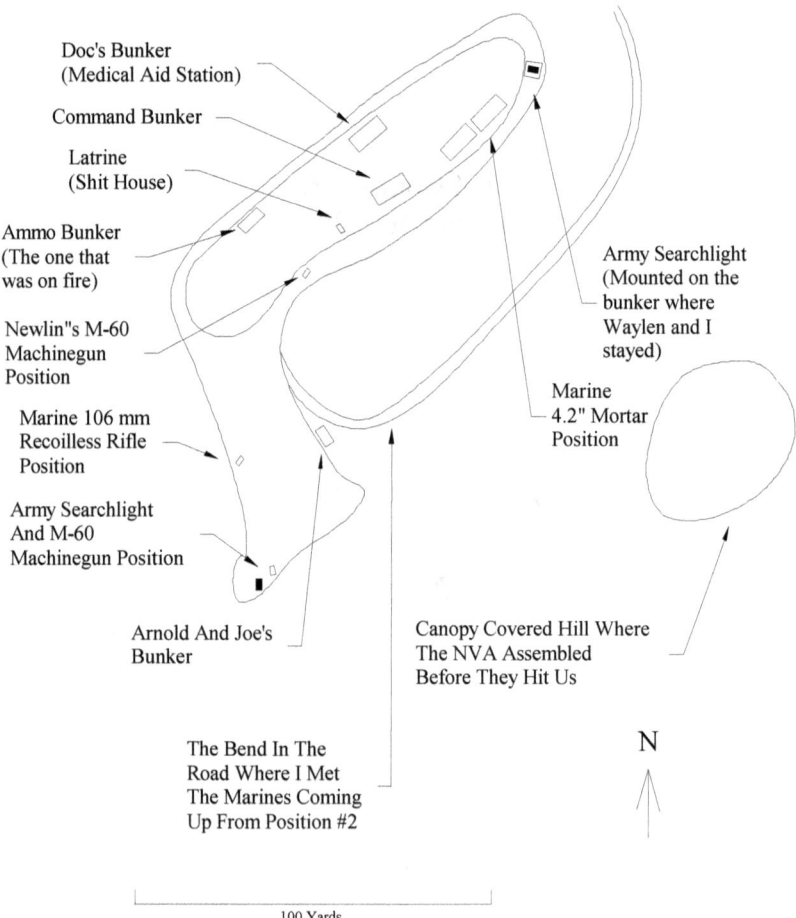

American Artillery And How It Works

The graphic on the next page shows how artillery is adjusted onto a target. Here's how it's done.

Military maps are laid out with grid lines at 1000-meter intervals. It's up to the observer to identify the target's location within the grid as a coordinate. Referencing the target from his position or a registration point can also do this, but a coordinate is the most common method. Based on the grid he would call in 38150, 82750 as the target location. This shows on the graphic as a dot. It indicates that the target is 150 meters north of grid 38, and 750 meters east of grid 82.

He would identify the target, North Vietnamese platoon in the open for example. Then select the type of round, H.E., high explosive, is normally used against troop positions.

He would probably use a timed fuse to create an Arial burst. Without overhead cover there is no protection from this kind of fuse.

The artillery battery would fire one round from the center of the battery, and the observer would adjust fire based on the location of the centered round. This is identified on the graphic as the First Round. In the example he would correct right 100, add 50. This correction is from his point of view. The Fire Direction Center converts this to corrections used by the firing battery.

Once the observer is satisfied he calls "Fire for effect." During his first call to the battery he identifies how many rounds he wants each artillery piece to fire. The battery is laid out so that the explosions overlap, covering a large area with deadly fire. The effect of artillery on troop positions is devastating.

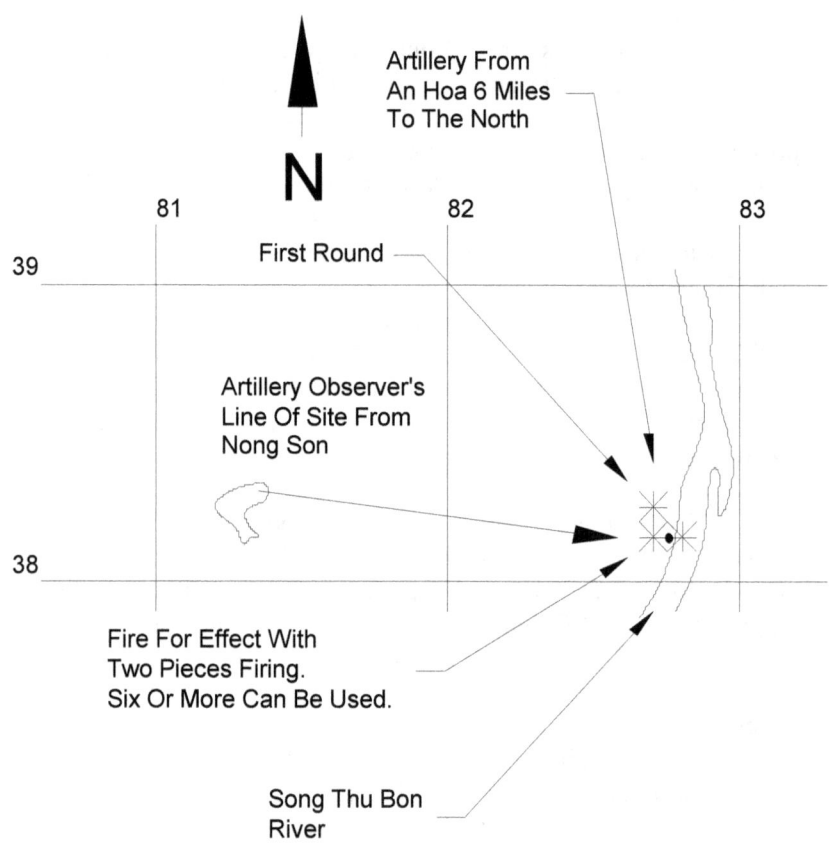

Bunker Construction

Bunkers were simply holes in the ground where we slept and stored our gear. They were not designed as fighting positions. There were no openings to fire from, and only one exit.

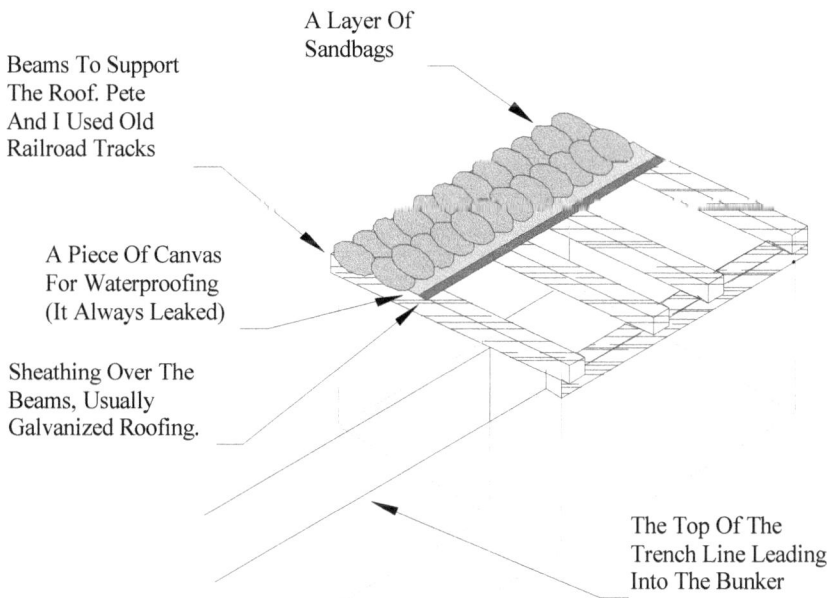

Inside The Bunker

The two-man bunker was set up with a shelf and a couple of cots with room underneath for storage. Each of us had waterproof bags for spare uniforms, and an extra pair of boots. It was important to check the bags before reaching in and the boots before putting them on. Rats and snakes liked to crawl inside.

Compared to the Marines, we lived in the lap of luxury. They carried all of their personal gear on their backs.

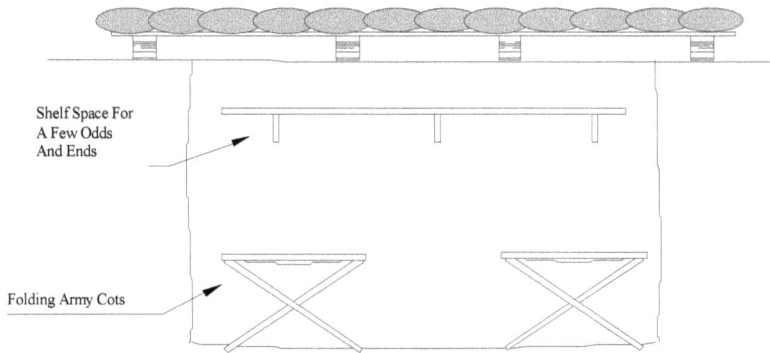

M-16 Rifle

The new M-16's had an incredibly high rate of fire. It gave each unit tremendous firepower. It also made it possible for each man to carry more ammunition. The high muzzle velocity caused serious wounds because of the extra energy released on impact.

The problem with it was it was very light weight, and not nearly as tough or accurate as the M-14's that we were issued in basic training. They were indestructible.

Bore: 5.56 mm
Rate of Fire:
    Cyclic – 800 rounds per min.
    Sustained – 12 to 15 rounds per min.
    Burst – 90 rounds per min.
Maximum effective range: 500 yards
Weight with 30 round magazine: 8.8 pounds

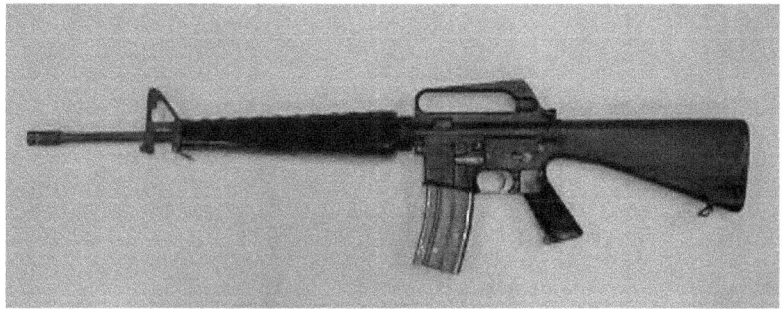

M-60 Machinegun

An Army Searchlight Section had a four-man crew, a section leader, assistant section leader, and two crewmen; each armed with an M-16. However, Its punch came from the M-60 machinegun. Each section had one. It was accurate and very dependable.

Bore: 7.62 mm
Rate of Fire:
    Cyclic – 550 rounds per min.
    Sustained – 100 rounds per min. (with barrel change every 100 rounds)
Maximum effective range: 1000 yards.
Weight: 18.75 pounds

Claymore Mine

Claymores were used extensively in Vietnam. The shaped charge threw shrapnel in a wide arc, and cut down anyone in its path.

Type: Fragmentation mine

Projectile: 700 steel spheres

Propellant: 1 ½ pounds of C-4 explosive

Detonation: Command detonated by a No.2 electric blasting cap.

Range:
    Kill zone- 50 meters
    Moderately effective to 100 meters
    Dangerous to 250 meters

Hand Grenade

We used grenades as a defensive weapon. While stationed at Namo Bridge we'd drop them into the water to keep the Vietnamese from using the river to approach our position. Dropping them into caves and tunnels ensured that no one was lurking below.

Type: Fragmentation

Delivery: Thrown by hand 30 to 50 yards

Range:
    Killzone-5 meters
    Effective zone-15 meters
    Danger zome-200 meters

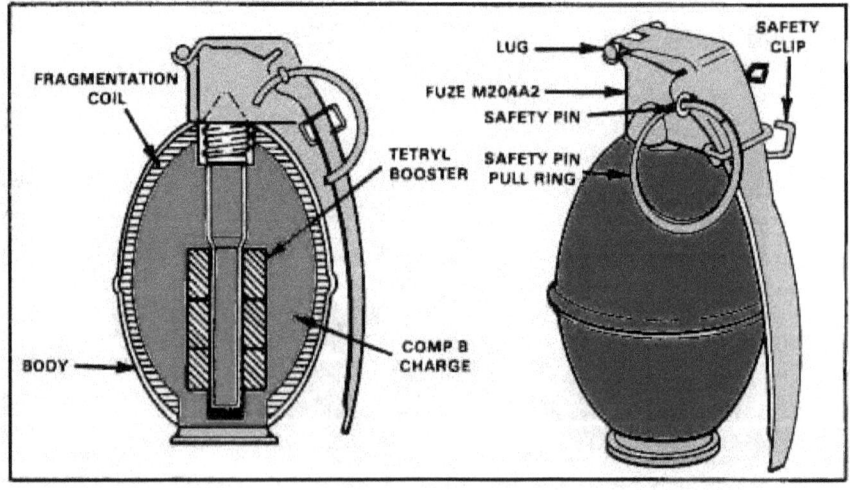

M61 fragmentation grenade.

Jeep
¼ *Ton*

This was our workhorse. It carried our gear and us wherever we went. It supplied power to the searchlight and our radio through out the night. These jeeps were unbelievably tough, and required very little maintenance.

The large searchlight was mounted behind the front seats, and took up all of the area in the back of the vehicle.

105mm Howitzer

This artillery piece was the smallest of the three howitzers that supported operations in the area around An Hoa. Although it could reach targets as far away as Nong Son, our position was at the far end of its seven mile range.

The An Hoa battery also had 155mm and 8" howitzers. The 8" not only packed a tremendous punch, but was the most accurate artillery piece in the world.

Picture Pages

*My Two Jeeps
With Searchlights Mounted
In The Back*

Helicopters Based At An Hoa
They Saved Countless Lives

Fire Mission
An Hoa 105mm Howitzer

Back In The Field South Of Da Nang

Fan Firing
We Tried To Fire Every Weapon As Often As Possible To Make Sure Everything Worked

Riding Shotgun
We Were Usually Part Of Convoy Security Whenever We Moved Because We Carried An M-60

Marines Moving Off The Landing Zone On Nong Son

Another Long Night
Manning The Lights

With Men Of Honor
By Doug Francescon
G Battery, 29th Artillery, U.S. Army
Who Proudly Served With
Fox Company, 2nd Battalion, 5th Marines
1st Marine Division

Rain on a wet poncho as I hugged my knees to my chest, trying to stay warm
Whispered voices and clicks on the radio as the ambushes and listening posts checked in
The thud of four duce mortars and the roar of a 106 recoilless rifle
Helicopter blades pounding the air at the LZ as wounded were carried off to DaNang
The roar from Puff's guns as they ripped through the jungle and the Vietnamese

These were the sounds burned into my memory as I stood with men of honor by my side.

Mist hanging over the river and valley below as the morning sun appeared
The dirt covered mountaintop with sand bagged bunkers and trenches cut into its surface
Thin tired faces, dirt covered flack jackets, and sweat soaked uniforms of my brothers
Eerie green shapes from the pitch black night in the eyepiece of infrared binoculars
My brothers lying in rows on the LZ, waiting for their last helicopter ride home

These were the sites burned into my memory as I stood with men of honor by my side.

Cold, lonely, endless nights trying not to think of family, home and friends so far away

The warmth and comfort of my brother's laughter when there was nothing to laugh about
The damp cold and suffocating heat that penetrated to the center of my bones
The confusion and despair as my dragon turned me into a heartless killer
The emptiness as I looked into the lifeless face of my best friend

These were the feelings burned into my memory as I stood with men on honor by my side.

The people in the airport back home who moved away and avoided me as they passed
Family and friends who didn't know the killer who returned from Vietnam
My hometown where I no longer fit, the one I had to leave
Drinking alone, unable to find anyone who understood or could relate
Moving from place to place, trying to find something that made sense

This was what I found when I left the men of honor by my side.

We were all so young and full of life with our whole future ahead
Each of us had the same dreams as those who stayed behind
But our dreams became clouded and very hard to find
These dreams were mixed with memories of blood and pain and death
Memories that stay with us all the years of our lives

This was the legacy of the men of honor by my side.

We had no homeland to welcome us back
Few understood and fewer cared
We seldom spoke of the war, no one wanted to hear
We struggled to bury memories that will always return
We fought to control the killer who lurked inside

We were left with nothing but each other, the men of honor by my side.

We weren't in Vietnam to defend our homeland because we hadn't been attacked
We didn't fight for riches, power, or glory; we fought only to stay alive
We risked our lives to save our brothers as they risked theirs for us
We grew close to one another because one another was all we had
There was no justification for our suffering, no reasons for the losses

So why was I sent to Vietnam with those men of honor by my side.

I will never find a reason although I've searched for many years
But, what I've found amazes me because it went unnoticed for so long
It's the common men, my brothers, who did such extraordinary things
Those fine young men who walked through hell each and every day
And I'm filled with pride and am privileged to say

THAT I STOOD WITH MEN OF HONOR BY MY SIDE

To My Brothers In Arms, Veterans Of The Vietnam War

If this finds its way to you please understand that it's my way of saying how proud I am to have served with you so many year ago. I hope that each of you finds peace and happiness all the rest of your days.

After all these years I take satisfaction in the fact that our effort and sacrifice was one of the few worthwhile parts of the Vietnam conflict. We were true to one another and ourselves.

Our nation turned its back as our blood was spilled as if we were somehow to blame for the losses, and that troubled me for many years. I, like so many, truly love this nation and what I thought it stood for.

I've put that disappointment behind me. Now I think only of you, the men I call my brothers, the ones who gave so much and received so little. I've always known that something good comes from everything; and this veteran's only reward was having stood with men like you.

Your Buddy,
Doug

Shadows From My Past

By Doug Francescon

Shadows dance across the wall from light the moon provides.
My wife lies sleeping quietly, close here by my side.
This should be a time of peace for me, a time to sleep and dream
Of happy times with those I love, and joys the future brings.

Instead I lay on sweat soaked sheets even though the room is cool
And try to gain control of what torments my heart and soul.
What reason can there be for this, the power that haunts my life
That keeps me from those happy times, and joys the future brings.

This haunting came from nowhere one cold and lonely night
As I walked the hall of my peaceful home with no one else inside.
This force that came upon me takes all my strength and will
To stay in touch with happy times, and joys the future brings.

So, why am I so troubled in these years that should be mine
These later years when I could return to joys I'd set aside
A time in life I've earned with toil and sweat and pain
When I could capture happy times, and joys the future brings.

At first I simply told myself "ignore it, it will pass"
This momentary trauma like other setbacks cannot last.
But as I regained control, and began to feel at ease
The trauma would return and block the joys the future brings.

So now I search the past for what has caused my deep unrest
But often find my heart and soul block my urgent quest
So much of me is turned away from what I must confront
The things that keep me from my peace and joys the future brings.

I have so much to live for. This world can bring great joy
To those who can appreciate its beauty and its peace.
So I must confront my demons however ugly they may be
And claim all of my happy times and joys the future brings.

The answers lie inside, deep in my heart and soul
Where I buried them so long ago so that I could carry on
I need not dig them out. Releasing them's the key
To casting off my burdens, and finding joys the future brings.

The answer comes from faith and love and courage I must find
Let down my guard's what I must do to allow what's locked inside
To stand before me in full view where I can identify
These hidden demons who block my peace and joys the future brings.

Facing them can be no worse than avoiding them has been
What err the confrontation brings will release my heart and soul
So I stand and face my gruesome past with one single goal in mind
To fully claim my happy times and joy the future brings.

Center
By,
Doug Francescon

Find your center they said, it's the only way
To know peace, satisfaction and joy
If you don't get in touch with that part of yourself
Then your life has no meaning or worth

What in the hell are you telling me now
Bout this center you say that I have?
And where in the hell do I find this great thing?
And why in the hell should I care?

It's the part of you where your memories are kept
Both the good and also the bad.
They went on to explain there are many more things
That reside there that cause who you are.

It's the place where you'll find what you felt on your heart
On the days that your children were born
Where you stored all the pride and the joy and the love
As they grew independent and strong

Tucked away in a special corner you'll see
The look in your own lover's eyes
As your lives intertwined and you two became one
Both the better for what you became.

Take your time as you look at the beauty that's there,
The great things that your eyes have beheld,
Sunrises over high mountain peaks,
And rainbows that follow spring showers.

You'll see there a picture of you as you faced
Heartache and sorrow and pain
You'll see too in that picture the pride you attained
As you concurred your fears and the pain

There are other things there that you must also see
For they're part of you just like the rest
Dark evil things that tour at your soul
And caused heartbreak and deep, sad unrest

Parents may find there a child that they lost,
Soldiers the horror of war
Lost love, failed careers, and all of the things
That none of us wants to endure.

So how do I find the joy in this place?
Was the question I could not ignore
When it's filled with all of the worst in my life
Block it out may be better by far.

Turning back from your center may keep you from pain
And anguish you've already seen.
But, protecting yourself will certainly cause
Loss of touch with the best life can bring.

Face the pain and the anguish and cry if you need
Then turn back to the best from your past
Delight in the joy and enjoy your success
For these things are too precious to hide.

Then open your heart to the world all around
Let your center take in all it can.
Both the good and the bad will come flooding in
Life brings all to each woman and man.

You must visit your center as much as you can
Sorting out all the bad from the good.
It is truly a window you cannot ignore.
It's the portal to each person's soul.

Special Note.
This last poem is for dad's everywhere, veterans or not. Being a husband and father gave my life meaning and purpose, and provided reasons to carry on when nothing else made sense.

The Broken Dryer
By:
Doug Francescon, Fortunate Husband and Proud Father / Grandfather

The dryers broken, it just blows cold air
Like when the what-ya-may-call-it went bad
I know that you're tired, but I need it real fast
We'll be out of clean cloths very soon.

Babe Ruth Baseball called this morning again.
They said you promised to coach one more year.
Our boys and their friends are counting on you
Without you they'll split up the team.

Are you limping again, on that same bad right leg?
Is it the knee or angle this time?
You should try to stay off it, and rest those old bones
Can you bring up some wood for the fire?

So, he tightens his boots, and turns toward the door
As he smiles at the woman he loves
She'll be busy with dinner for an hour or so
Enough time for the wood and the dryer.

Hi Dad, he hears his young daughter say
As her greeting brightens his day
It only takes a word or two
And he forgets the pain in his knee.

He bends and grabs the splitting maul
As he heads for pile of logs
"This won't take long" He says to himself.
As his wife warns. "Be careful out there."

Another broad smile crosses his face
As he considers her warning and fears
"A man lost a toe using one of those things."
She continues with concerns so sincere.

"I read about him in the paper today,"
He calls back to his wife from the yard
Then says to himself. "He'd have a full set of toes.
If he'd kept his head out of his ass."

The seasoned wood pieces fly both left and right
As he drives the maul out and then down.
It feels good to allow his muscle and brawn
To serve him as they were intended serve.

In a very short time he's unloading a pile
Of newly spit wood for the fire
With plenty of time for the dryer that failed
Cause it's been overloaded again.

He's replaced burned out elements so often that now
He could change them with both eyes closed tight.
Once or twice he suggested they lighten the loads
To help lengthen the new coil's life.

One evening he even tried to explain
How important air flow can be
And how electric components need it
To keep cool how they were intended to be.

Though the warning fell on deaf ears once again
Like so many warnings before.
He knows it's important to try
And hell maybe someday someone will hear.

But until that day comes he'll continue to fix
Dryers and mowers and cars
And be there to guide and council and coach
Because he's a man and a father who cares.

Reflections And Realizations

It's been six years sense the first printing of this book. So far we have distributed copies through out the United States, and have them as far away as Australia. My greatest satisfaction has been comments from families of veterans who say that they now understand loved ones who have faced war much better than before. And, that, as much as anything else, was why I wrote the book.

During the past four years I attended reunions of both Fox Company, 2/5 Marines and G Battery, 29th Artillery. The guys from 2/5 did me the honor of allowing me to read my poem, "Men Of Honor." Doing so brought me closer to those fine men for whom I have the greatest respect. I have also visited my home town, Rock Island, Illinois where I was able to spend time with Bob and Judy Blomgren and Nanette Sheley who is married to a Vietnam veteran who served with Special Forces.

Contact with those people from my past opened a whole new world for me, and was the greatest factor in the final healing process. Bob and Judy showed me that life goes on. Through them I saw that love and happiness still exist no mater what personal disasters occur. While with them I found the same love and friendship that I once knew. All I had to do was reach out for it. When I did the dragon went sound to sleep. They showed me that love never dies; fools like me just turn their back on it.

Nanette was my window back to the person I once was, and wanted to be again. As I talked with her I became that relaxed, free and easy guy that once had such a keen eye for the most beautiful things in life. As I talked with her husband, Bob, I saw in him a reflection of a part of me. It was the same reflection I saw in the guys from Fox Company and G Battery. It let me know I wasn't alone.

Through all this my wife, Pati, stayed by my side, giving me the time, love and understanding I needed to work things out. I feel that I've finally come home and found Pati waiting for me. I'm a very lucky man.

I now see my children and grandchildren in a new light. During the hard times when nothing made sense, they gave my life purpose. My love for them kept me sober, and got me out the door and off to work every day. Without my wife and kids I'd have found no reason to keep trying.

Dealing with the war and the effect it had on my life truly made me a better man. I'm amazed that some good can come from a hell hole like Vietnam. God truly works in mysterious ways. I know he never left my side.